A NOTE TO TEACHERS AND PARENTS:

This is no official history or record of high-level strategy by some commanding admiral. It is the very personal story of a very junior naval lieutenant, flying a navy torpedo bomber. He does nothing spectacular, nor is he a professional writer. But this book has the ring of truth about it.

Mears begins his story on the lazy Sunday morning of December 7th, when Pearl Harbor was suddenly attacked, and ends it a year later. During this time, we are with him through every drink he takes, every joke his fellow fliers crack, and every time he stands on deck and realizes that another buddy is not coming back from his flight.

In the midst of the battle for Midway and the battle of Guadalcanal, Pilot Mears did not know what was happening and, since the reader is always with him, we do not know either. But we do know what the wind feels like as it sweeps over an empty flight deck; what it is like to get up at dawn on the day your squadron is to make its first combat flight; and what it is like to stand on the flight deck, as the reserve pilot left behind, and realize that not a single plane of your squadron's fifteen survived its first five minutes in combat.

As in other books of this series, written by young combat pilots on the other side, *Kamikaze, Samurai,* and *Stuka Pilot* (Bal Hi Nos: U2821, U2806, U2823), every moment in this account is true. The originality and worth of this story however, is that all the events happened to a very young man who put it down exactly as he felt it. In this generation, when most of our actual combat fighting and dying is being done by boys little more than eighteen and is being read about by boys a few years younger, it is important to remember that the very young do not approach fighting and killing and dying with the same attitude as the middle-aged, the veterans, or the old generals.

Young Lieutenant Mears' first view of the wounds of dead

men on the flight deck surprises him. He had seen death in the movies but had never realized that the muscles and sinews showed so vividly through the blood. In spite of this, all the young officers could think about was the excitement of flying a combat mission. They come back from their first ones excited and joking and desperately eager to go out again. It reminds the reader of boys who have just discovered a thrill-packed snow slope for their sleds. They discover that "it was fun bombing!", that grieving over your friends who were killed each day takes effort and it is much better to concentrate on the facts and figures of your job. When Mears' closest buddy is lost on a flight, Mears admits that it took him almost a whole day of moping to get over it! The commander he admires most is the one who led his fifteen planes into an attack that he knew beforehand would be suicide for the squadron. In another incident, every one forgives the pilot who kills himself stunting around before landing on the deck because, after all, fighter pilots are supposed to be full of high spirits, "and if they get killed, that's their own business."

For these brave young flyers it was a Gilbert and Sullivan operetta war, fought with jokes and anecdotes about admirals falling into the water. Only in a few places does old-fashioned realism darken the boyish high jinks of this book: for instance in the occasional aside when the author remarks that, of his ten or fifteen friends whom he has been describing, only two or three are still alive one year later; and in the publisher's note on the first page, indicating that the author was killed in the line of duty six months after the book ends.

Richard H. Tyre
Chairman, English Department
Germantown Friends School

CARRIER COMBAT

Frederick Mears, Lieut., U.S.N.R.

BALLANTINE BOOKS   •   NEW YORK

IRS: Page 112

"A big fire was sending . . . a destroyer was firing toward Guadalcanal."

To

DICK JACCARD

and

JAMIE DEXTER

PUBLISHERS' NOTE

On June 28, 1943, shortly after Lieutenant Mears had completed this book, his publishers were informed that Frederick Mears had been killed in line of duty. Word was also received at that time that Lieutenant Frederick Mears had been posthumously awarded the Distinguished Flying Cross, which had been issued to him prior to his death but which had not been received by him before he died.

CITATION:

"For heroism and extraordinary achievement in aerial combat against enemy Japanese forces in the Solomon Islands on October 3 and 5, 1942. Participating in a raid launched by three torpedo bombers against a force of hostile warships proceeding toward Guadalcanal, Lieutenant (junior grade) Mears, boldly striking at the enemy with four 500-pound bombs, contributed to the aggregate score of two direct hits which set a Japanese cruiser aflame, and one near-miss on a destroyer. When he returned to strafe the cruiser, an enemy shell-burst ripped a hole in the fuselage of his plane and critically wounded his bomber. Two days later he took off in a flight of five bombers, twelve scout bombers and one Flying Fortress to raid Rekata Bay on Santa Isabel Island. As one of the nine surviving planes to reach their objective, Lieutenant (junior grade) Mears, although unable to release his bomb load, vigorously strafed Japanese ground installations in the face of tremendous fire from both enemy aircraft and shore batteries. By his aggressive fighting spirit and skillful airmanship on these two flights he enabled his gunners to shoot down a total of three planes."

For the President,
FRANK KNOX
Secretary of the Navy

FOREWORD

THE BOYS on a carrier lead a good life. On board they struggle with the sea, the sun, and the wind—and the Japs. Ashore they wink at anyone's girl and take her if they can. This is a tale of how some of them flew and fought from San Francisco to Rabaul.

CONTENTS

INTRODUCTION

THE FOLLOWING CHAPTERS are not primarily devoted to torpedo plane warfare. They form a narrative of a group of naval aviators who left the States a few months after December 7, 1941, to deal with "that unpleasantness in the Pacific." Nevertheless, since much of the combat action described involves torpedo planes, a short take of present-day aircraft sending home their "fish with wings" will help the reader to understand the engagements and to visualize the nature of a torpedo attack.

"Suicide" is the word most used to describe the intention of the torpedo plane pilot. Ever since Midway, when three squadrons of naval heroes flew their outmoded aircraft to annihilation to sink Jap carriers, the torpedo plane has been thought of as a flying coffin.

This conception is no longer true. A new and faster aircraft with superior armament, the Grumman Avenger, has replaced the Douglas Devastator (which itself was ahead of the field when it was accepted by the Navy in the middle thirties). The Avenger is rated the best torpedo plane of any navy in the world.

Once equipped with a fast plane, the Navy developed different tactics for the torpedo attack, including close co-ordination with dive bombers and protection by fighters. A new torpedo, carrying a war head with more TNT capable of being dropped at higher air speeds and faster in the water, was put in service. With these improvements as a basis for their work, fresh torprons (torpedo squadrons) took to the air with better chances of getting hits and of getting away after they had slipped their wienies into Jap warships.

The tactics practiced by our torprons are still "wide open," and those that have been frozen are confidential. There are as many different ideas as to how a torpedo attack should be made as there are torpedo plane pilots.

In general, however, on a daylight raid with unlimited ceiling the torpedo planes scatter after an approach from altitude and spread out fanwise ahead of the ship selected for destruction in an attempt to bracket both bows. Then if the torpedoes strike the sea at short intervals the enemy vessel meets a nest of converging wakes, each a telltale line tracing the course of a potential deathblow. If she turns in one direction attempting to "comb" one group of torpedoes the others strike her broadside. There is no escape from such an ideal pattern. Jap warship captains are well aware of this, however, and before the torpedo squadron reaches the breakup point the Jap ships are circling, twisting, and maneuvering to foil a co-ordinated run on the bows.

The pilot of a torpedo plane approaching for an attack on a Jap task force first sees black puffs of heavy A.A. fire when he is still about five miles away. His leader meantime has been singling out the enemy vessel to be concentrated on and has chosen the path in through the screening vessels. Carriers, battleships, cruisers, and transports are the dish for the squadron's torpedoes, in that order. As the planes close in, the A.A. changes from puffball bursts to heavy-millimeter tracer fire— thin wisps of light coming up slowly from below and streaking past to soar overhead.

The squadron is at the breakup point now, and each pilot makes the rest of the trip alone amidst an increasing concentration of opposing fire. Destroyers and cruisers are pinking at him continuously, light machine gun fire has thrown a crazy web of tracers around his plane, the water below him is lashed to a froth with shellfire, and smoke is obscuring some of the ships from his eyes. Although he is traveling over 250 miles per hour, he seems to be standing still and thinks he almost could run faster.

Now his training begins to tell. His bomb bay doors are already open, for though this slows down the speed of the plane it insures that enemy gunfire will not jam the opening mechanism and make the trip useless. What the pilot is thinking about as he is automatically jinking, skidding, and turning through the fire is the selection of his dropping point. To determine this spot he must consider the speed of the ship and the angle of his plane to the course of the vessel.

When he finally reaches this imaginary spot he picks his lead—anywhere from one half to three ship lengths ahead of the target—and trips the button which releases his fish. At this point the plane is from 1,200 to 800 yards from the ship.

The modern torpedo is a highly developed instrument of devastation. When it falls from a plane traveling at high speed it strikes the water and begins the homing journey through the sea under its own power. Gyros keep it on a course identical to that of the plane at the drop.

Most torpedoes run true, but because they are such intricate mechanisms and are dropped from speeding aircraft in such a rough manner, many have erratic runs. A torpedo may run in circles or, if the pilot lets it go too high, flop over on a reverse course. If it is dropped too low it is apt to break when it hits the water. If the plane is not in straight and level flight when the fish leaves the bomb bay it may hook or broach and porpoise on top of the water. In addition to these eccentricities, the torpedo has a characteristic left hook when it enters the sea.

The pilot won't worry about what the torpedo does after it leaves the plane, however, interested though he may be. When he hears his bombardier call "Torpedo away" over the interphone and sees the red light in the cockpit blink off as the bomb bay doors are closed he knows that the most important part of his job is done.

The next part of his task, and it seems just as important to him, is to get himself and his crew out of the range of the A.A. fire without being shot down. The Grumman Avenger is a fast plane and a rugged plane, and usually it brings the boys through, with a few irregular shrapnel holes in the wings and fuselage perhaps, but still in the air heading home.

CARRIER COMBAT

1

Caught with Our Flaps Down

A GROUP OF YOUNG ENSIGNS, naval aviators, were sprawled in the roomy lounge of the junior officers' quarters at the San Diego Naval Air Station. It was a bright Sunday morning. They were stretched out on the carpet reading the funny papers and listening to the radio or sitting smoking and basking in the sunlight or just asleep altogether in leather chairs. Some were talking of the night before, but for the most part they weren't doing much of anything.

The day was December 7, 1941.

Among us that morning were Harry March, college track star and fighter pilot, who had two Jap planes to his credit the last time I saw him; Jim Shelton, of Great Falls, Montana, a dive bomber pilot last seen after attacking a Jap ship at Midway; Bill Pittman, a Florida boy who, week after week on the carrier, talked only of his girl, "Little Natalie"; Jamie Dexter, of Seattle, lost from the carrier two degrees from the equator and never found; Jerry Stablein, a big football player who delighted in making bucktooth faces and talking like a Jap; Hank Schneider, of Texas, who spun in off Diamond Head; Tom Durkin, survivor of fourteen days in a rubber boat in the Coral Sea; Bill Wileman, killed at Guadalcanal; Dick Jaccard, from Manhattan, Kansas, ace dive bomber, the gayest of us all, who planted a 1,000-pound bomb in the center of the flight deck of the Jap carrier *Akagi* and later died on the *Wasp*; Jerry Richey, of Denver, veteran pilot who always seemed to feel so strongly on every

19

subject and everybody we discussed; and Harry Frederickson, from Spokane, who kept the girls in Coronado running around in circles and who probably is in action right now somewhere in the Pacific.

There were others, too, whom I can't recall, but almost without exception the ensigns lazing about in the lounge that morning were to see violent action in the Pacific during the coming year. We were all members of an advanced carrier training group undertaking specialized instruction in service planes before joining operating squadrons in the fleet.

At about 11:00 A.M. (PST) the dreamy organ music on the radio cut out and an excited news commentator read us the first bulletin of the attack on Hawaii. All we learned was that "unidentified planes had made an attack on Pearl Harbor."

Foolish grins betrayed our initial excitement at this Orson Wellesian announcement, but our natural impulse to skepticism won out.

"Some dope dropped a smoke bomb on Waikiki Beach," one of us ventured.

"Army planes got lost again. I wonder if they jettisoned their bombs this time."

"Maybe a Jap admiral got a bug in his noggin and sent in an attack group."

We couldn't absorb the truth all at once, especially after the welter of confused and contradictory details that poured over the air during the remainder of the morning. Continuing reports roughly outlined the attack on Hawaii as having been made by unidentified aircraft dropping bombs on naval warships in Pearl Harbor, on Hickam Field, on Kaneohe Naval Air Station, on a residential district of Honolulu, and on Schofield Barracks, killing 350 American soldiers. A small group of parachutists were landed on one of the islands, bulletins affirmed. The radio hinted at future press censorship. As these reports filled the air it only gradually dawned on us that a major attack on Hawaii really had been effected.

Suddenly we realized that nobody knew anything about the Japs. We never had heard of a Zero then. What was the caliber of Jap planes and airmen? What was the strength of the Japanese Navy? What kind of battles would be fought and where? Apparently we were woefully unprepared, lacking planes and ships, and the Japs had struck hard. They had caught us in the landing circle with our flaps down.

As if waking from a long sleep, we slowly became aware of many facts that we hadn't thought about before: the difference of time in the Pacific; the importance of Alaska; the huge distances to be covered by attacking and defending forces; and the plight of Australia. Our conception of the Japs as ridiculous cameramen with buckteeth began to change, although we still didn't think of the new enemy as an intelligent and courageous foe.

We began to wonder what we would be doing next. The *Saratoga* was in port, and we thought the Navy might pack us all aboard and send the carrier to the islands. She was getting up steam. The *Enterprise* was due in two days.

No immediate action was taken so far as we were concerned until after lunch at about one o'clock, when we were ordered to report to flight headquarters in uniform. Sunday was usually a holiday and we had been allowed to wear civilian clothes off duty, but we discovered that henceforward we would be required to wear uniforms ashore.

At the hangar we were ordered to stand by. We wandered about among the planes watching ordnancemen loading new and fresh-looking 500-pound bombs under the bellies of the SBD Douglas dive bombers. We were a bewildered and still slightly disbelieving lot. We couldn't comprehend that there was no simple explanation for the attack and that the whole affair would not be smoothed over on the morrow.

During the afternoon varying reports of the radio press informed us that the Japs had attacked Hawaii but not Manila, taken Wake Island, bombed and surrounded Guam, attacked Hong Kong, and placed landing parties on Borneo and Australia. We didn't know what to believe. Announcements requested that all officers and men of the Army and Navy contact their stations.

As the evidence mounted during the evening that Jap action undoubtedly was backed by their Government, commentators had no doubt we would declare war on the morrow. We learned that Jap colonies in Los Angeles and

San Francisco and elsewhere on the Coast were being patrolled, air-raid spotting organizations mobilized, outbound shipping held on the Coast, and about 1,000 ships at sea ordered to return. The President met with his Cabinet.

For all practical purposes we were at war. In the short space of twelve hours the boys yawning in the lounge in the morning had become by evening men marked for combat within short weeks or months.

The next night, December 8, Lieutenant Gil Schlendering of the Marine Corps and I came out of the movies in San Diego and strolled up to the cocktail lounge of a hotel overlooking the city for a beer before going to bed. We were tasting our drinks and listening to the gowned entertainer tinkling the keys of the piano with "Harbor Lights" when the lights suddenly went out.

San Diego was undergoing its first blackout. The presence of fifty or sixty unidentified planes in the San Francisco area a few hours earlier was the reason.

The bartender lit candles and set them on the bar. In the flickering darkness we looked out over the city and saw the lights blink out in groups and one by one. It was impressive to see a great community in our country succumbing to the dark mantle of war for the first time. To Gil and me it was exciting, too. We peered out the windows and almost hoped to hear the sirens wail and the dull "whoompf" of bombs to complete the picture we had seen so many times in the movies.

We noticed also that many lights did not go out, in particular a large neon sign about two blocks down the street. The blackout was only partial and hence relatively ineffective.

The civilians in the bar were silent for the most part as they watched their town disappear into the night.

Gil and I drove off the ferry into a complete blackout in Coronado. There was no moon, and it was pitch-black. Cars were creeping along the streets with no lights at all or with parking lights which were fairly bright and then flashing on their head lamps as they approached each other. The Marine sentry at the gate at North Island stopped us and used a shielded red flashlight to examine our newly acquired passes.

Next morning the station was still under stand-by orders.

Most of us were doing no flying, but several of the officers who had been there longest were operating a patrol over the Pacific from an auxiliary field near the Mexican border. Larry Comer, who was one of these, said he was sent out at 2:30 o'clock that day, when a rumor that an enemy cruiser was off the coast came through. They flew out in formation in bumpy air with snow packing past the cockpit. Spotting some vessel in the storm and being unable to identify it, they climbed to 8,000 feet, strung out into a line, and dove but dropped no bombs. The flight leader had decided the ship was friendly. Comer said he was sent out again in the same soup as soon as he returned. Evidently the Navy was not sparing pilots who were experienced enough to operate over the sea in such nasty weather.

During the first week of the war there were feverish preparations both on the station and in San Diego to meet any wartime actuality which might develop. On the station, the windows of the hangars and of most of the buildings in use at night were given a coat of black paint as a permanent way of preventing light escaping during the blackout. Sailors and Marines busied themselves digging zigzag trenches about four feet deep to be used as bomb shelters, and these made jagged scars all over the base. Circular anti-aircraft pits protected by sandbags and housing .50-caliber machine guns were dug at intervals around the field. Sentries on the alert challenged constantly, especially at night. The training planes were scattered around the edge of the field about 300 feet apart, and the regular service planes were chocked in dirt revetments to shield them from bomb splinters.

Across the channel San Diegoans were warned by the Civilian Defense Council to turn off home and car lights when the street lights went out, to stay at home as much as possible in the evening, to remain calm in the event of any raid. They were told that air-raid alarms would consist of the sounding of fire sirens throughout the city.

There was good reason for the intensity with which those on the west coast pursued these defensive measures during the early days of the war. Many air-raid alarms were broadcast in San Francisco and Los Angeles when unidentified planes appeared overhead. Merchant ships reported having been attacked by Jap subs off the coast. The large Japanese population in cities and farms on the coastland presented a sabotage threat.

But after the first week or ten days of the war the fever began to subside. As the scares and alarms one after another turned out to be false and the civilians began to realize that, after all, a good many miles of water separated us from Japan, they slacked off and took things a little easier. We noticed that they stopped clapping us on the back and treating us like heroes and telling us to "get one for me, brother." As Tom Durkin said, "I guess we'll have to start buying our own drinks again."

We became bored with the war also. There was no tangible evidence of it. We could still eat as heartily as we wished, go to good movies, read peacefully in bed, sit in a bar or dance with an attractive girl when we were off duty. At that time there was little flying, since we were waiting to start an intensive six weeks' training course which would make us ready to go to the fleet. Therefore our superior officers granted us regular overnight liberty and, after eight days of war, allowed us the week ends off also.

On the Saturday after Pearl Harbor Jamie Dexter and two other officers and I were driving back from an evening in San Diego. We stopped at an intersection for a red light, and shortly two girls in a long swish Packard drew alongside. We began to chat with them, and very soon we had parked our car and all climbed into theirs. They suggested that we drive to Tijuana, Mexico, and, although it was against regulations to cross the border, it didn't take us long to decide that was the only place to go.

We had no trouble getting over the line, because we took off our hats and hid them in the bottom of the car, rolled our sleeves to cover our ensign stripes, and acted for the border officials like high-school boys in blue serge out for a Saturday night frolic—which wasn't hard at the time.

After wheeling into the neon glow of Tijuana's main street, we parked and then jammed ourselves into the Aloha, one of the Mexican honky-tonks which line the avenue. To speak in the vernacular, the joint was jumping. We couldn't get a table for about three quarters of an hour and in the meantime stood at the bar drinking tequila and talking to the Mexicans. They didn't seem to know just who we were or why we were there, but they were quite friendly nevertheless. Several, because we had wings, thought we were in the R.A.F. To most the war was far away, and they were entirely passive about it. The natives we talked to appeared slovenly and lackadaisical but were having a good time in a carefree, childish manner. Their clothes were old and sometimes tattered and they themselves poorly groomed. We felt conspicuous and unnecessary in our uniforms until we were able to get a table and watch the feather dancer. She had a delicious little body, and I sent her a soiled gardenia and a drink, inviting her to come over, but no potatoes. All in all, our visit to Mexico was not a total washout, although we did come back with the impression that our little brown friends south of the border were not going to be much help in this conflict.

A few days after Christmas about twenty of us in the advanced carrier training group were ordered to Terminal Island, San Pedro, near Long Beach. We were to fly anti-submarine patrols in the *Kingfisher,* a scout-observation plane (OS2U-2). Marine Lieutenant Jack Foeller and I drove up the coast in an old Ford I had purchased and escaped with only two flats on the way. The gentle green slopes along the coastline flecked with bright-colored roofs reminded me in my imagination of the shorelines of Italy and Greece (which I had never seen). A sea breeze kept the drive refreshing until we began to approach Long Beach, where the hills are forested with oil derricks and the stench of the crude oil is sweet and nauseous.

Flying at Terminal Island consisted of flying up the Channel on the prowl for subs. Each plane was loaded with two 100 pound bombs and fitted with machine guns. None of us ever found a periscope, but more than once we flung a bomb at a school of fish or a shadow in the water. One or two planes would pick up and follow a convoy for several hours as the ships headed for the open sea. We circled them continually in a designated pattern, watching for enemy subs, looking the individual ships over, and wondering toward what port they were bound. When it came time to take our leave we passed between the ships, rocking our wings to wish them luck, and then set course for the base.

The first plane I flew from Terminal Island had faulty air-speed, altitude, and rate-of-climb indicators, and I had some little difficulty flying it at first. I took off in the dark and nosed up and out over the water. Glancing at my air-speed, I noted that it registered thirty knots, considerably below stalling speed. "Yipe!" I almost jumped out of the cockpit, because a plane absolutely will not fly unless it maintains a certain speed. Instead, however, I nosed over and picked up considerable velocity. My air-speed meter still indicated thirty knots, and I knew then it was out. Trusting to the fact that the plane seemed to have plenty of speed and that I was experiencing no stall symptoms, I began to climb slowly. When I thought I was at about 1,000 feet my altimeter read 200 feet and my rate-of-climb indicator, 3,000 feet up. My confusion was aggravated by the predawn darkness and by the fact that this was one of the few times I had flown over the sea, which presents a different aspect than land panorama. The only flight instrument I had in operation was my turn and bank indicator, which is of no value in determining altitude and air-speed.

We had been trained to believe our flight instruments almost implicitly, since they are usually correct and the impressions of the pilot who flies by the "seat of his pants" more often than not are wrong. As soon as I knew I wasn't going to spin in, however, I forced myself away from this training habit; and gradually, by using my engine instruments, all of which were operating normally, I was able to establish a constant air-speed and altitude. Specifically, I set the throttle and propeller pitch control to maintain cruising manifold pressure and r.p.m. and adjusted the tabs for level flight. I was glad of this chance to work out such an emergency system, because I felt the need for practice in meeting the unusual situations which crop up in the combat area.

All of us had a gay holiday season at San Pedro. For some reason the girls in Long Beach were more susceptible to uniforms than in San Diego. Perhaps there were more girls or fewer servicemen, or perhaps the population around Los

Angeles was nearer to the war because the area was a more likely place for the enemy to strike. At any rate, on our evening frolics we found a wide and fascinating choice of frills and perfume.

On New Year's Eve, Harry March and I, with two Marine lieutenants, Ken Kirk and Pete McGlothlin, left Terminal Island to investigate Hollywood. I guess we had in mind meeting a few of the downy starlets and beautiful but poverty-stricken extra girls that are supposed to abound in filmland. It doesn't matter, because we never did get far enough to satisfy our curiosity. We stopped at a little corner bar outside of Los Angeles and had several rounds to grease the wheels. The manager bought us one or two more. When we left there we decided to stop at the nearest and gaudiest night club we drove by and begin the evening's operations. The first we came across was the Florentine Gardens, in Los Angeles. We paid the enormous cover charge and entered the arena, sat down at a table, and for a time watched the blondes on the stage flashing their flesh at the ringside tables. This became tedious for our mood, and we adjourned to the bar—or, rather, to join the ladies, for the cocktail lounge was crowded with them, most, in the terms of hot-spot owners, "unescorted." The four of us were like donkeys between a number of haystacks—we didn't know which to choose—so we stood at the bar and had several stiff drinks and then picked those nearest to us.

I saw these three boys after they had spent several months in the South Pacific, and they all agreed that anyone who didn't appreciate the varied pleasures a woman adds to a man's existence hasn't been without one very long or else is a damn fool. There are other things such boys miss too—good food, drinks, books, up-to-the-minute news, and their parents—but most of all women.

On our return to San Diego we began an intensive six weeks' training course in the Douglas dive bomber preparatory to going to the fleet. We were divided into a Blue Squadron and a Red Squadron, each with eighteen pilots, and began flying about six hours a day seven days a week. Flights over a sector 150 miles out to sea taught us to get used to flying out of sight of shore; landing on a narrow strip of field by following the directions of a signal officer helped us master the routine of landing on a carrier deck; and gunnery hops introduced us to the chattering power of our machine guns.

We flew formation at night, keeping position on the ghostly outline of the next plane by the light of the exhaust flare. We had more Link trainer hops in the ingenious sweatbox which teaches airmen on the ground what it will be like to fly on instruments when they get in the air. Later on we actually flew up into the clouds and experienced that panicky moment when the pilot knows he's on his back in an inverted spin and the instruments tell him he is in a steep climb to the left.

On one of the several oxygen or altitude hops that we took, Dick Rugen, flying at 20,000 feet, suddenly slumped over in a faint from lack of oxygen. Fortunately, his plane was well trimmed and fell off into a shallow glide. He regained consciousness at about 17,000 feet. His wingman, Joe Sanders, didn't realize Rugen was out and kept his position on the pilotless craft throughout.

An oxygen mask, necessary as it is, is an uncomfortable apparatus the first few times it is used. It seems to stifle and suffocate rather than relieve the function of breathing. Unless it is properly put on, dust particles from the filter catch in the pilot's lungs. The mask worries the wearer's nose. Moisture from the breather fills the rubber well with slobber. The pilot usually aggravates the irritation by breathing too heavily, and the surplus air pushes out around the sides of the filter. All in all, the device which allows the flier to live high above his normal medium takes a great deal of the joy out of sailing about in the light blue sky so far above the earth.

We had innumerable dive-bombing flights and after two weeks were able to lay a miniature smoke bomb inside a 200-foot stationary target on every dive without fail. To qualify we had to put four bombs within a 50-foot radius of the bull's eye. Practice dive-bombing is not as exciting to the pilot as one might believe, because he is busy with too many of the details of flying the plane. Before the dive he is concerned with his throttle, propeller pitch control, super-charger, with cracking his diving flaps (to slow the plane down in the dive) and setting his switches. During the long rush downward he must concentrate on keeping his pipper (the center of his sight) on the target by twisting and corkscrewing the plane, on estimating the drift of the plane caused by the wind, and on preparing to pull the bomb release. The thrill of acceleration as the plane picks up speed in its headlong drop straight for the earth is not entirely lost, though, and most pilots enjoy this training.

Combat dive-bombing is another story. Pilots who have gone down on maneuvering enemy ships say that in addition to the mechanics of operating the plane they must think about evading enemy fighters, confusing the A.A. gunners aboard by jinking in the dive, and putting the bomb where the ship will be, not where it is. More often than not dive bombers in the fleet do not split their flaps, and consequently they pick up much more speed. Moreover, they usually come down from higher levels than in practice bombing.

When this training period began six of us moved into a house in Coronado which we called the Wolf Farm (because we had become tired of hearing such establishments referred to as snake ranches). Jamie Dexter, Jerry Richey, Bruce Ek, Harry Frederickson, Bob Vaupell, and myself lived there in a luxurious manner with a maid and a number-one boy to prepare and serve the best food and drinks we could buy.

In those last weeks before we went to sea we watched our friends depart suddenly, sometimes after only twenty-four hours' notice. A farewell party was always in order, and all of us had as gay a time in that period as our flying duties would allow.

Bruce Ek and Bob Vaupell, who were both Marines, left late in January. Bruce was a tall, blond athlete, extremely well built and good-looking, an archetype of the Marine flier. Because of his looks and devil-may-care manner he was seemingly irresistible to women. Bruce gave to Coronado his "KO for Tokyo," a sledge-hammer drink consisting of two jiggers of bourbon whisky, one of rum, one of gin, one of French vermouth, and one of Italian vermouth. Mixed in a large highball glass with ice and decorated with a thin slice of lemon peel, it was surprisingly smooth but packed an awful wallop and was responsible for the downfall of more than one girl. When Bruce left a cute little girl in Coronado and another in San Diego both considered themselves heartbroken. We missed his friendliness and good humor. Bruce later was killed at Midway when, as those on the island said, he attacked two Jap Zeros in his dive bomber.

Bob Vaupell, who had moved out of our Wolf Farm to get married, left his bride of a week to put to sea with Bruce. Fortunately, he returned less than a year later with a wound in the leg which he got while being chased for miles all alone by more than twenty Zeros.

My sister, whose husband is a navy doctor, arrived from Honolulu with her two small children shortly after Bruce and Bob left. She was absolutely mum about what had happened at Pearl Harbor and refused to give me any details of December 7. I tried plying her with cocktails and reciting to her the worst rumors I had heard, but she wouldn't crack. She said passengers aboard the transport had been given strict orders not to say anything to anybody. She was thoroughly inculcated with the seriousness of the war and was amazed at the offhand manner in which people in the States seemed to take it.

Ensign Jim Daniels, fighter pilot, returned from the war zone in February and gave us our first eyewitness account of the Marshall and Gilbert Islands raids. Daniels was on a carrier which took part in the attack. The planes took off before dawn, he said, and bombed Jap hangars and strafed planes dispersed on the ground. Daniels said he went down to 700 feet to drop his bombs on a hangar, which "rose up and disintegrated in the air," and then returned to strafe enemy personnel who were completely surprised and running for cover. Later in the day he tangled with a Jap fighter plane which had succeeded in taking off. The two planes hurtled head on at each other, the Jap turning on his back to keep his sights on Daniels, but the latter did the better shooting and flew off the victor.

The most astonishing thing about the raid as far as his carrier was concerned was the fact that it cruised up and down not twenty miles from the objective, almost within full view of the enemy, in order to be able to send in as many attacks as possible.

The Japs pressed home a retaliatory bombing attack in the afternoon, scoring one hit. A flaming Jap bomber tried to crashland on the deck, but just as it seemed the plane must hit the carrier the captain turned the ship out from under.

Individual incidents which Daniels described included the feat of a fighter pilot who flew his plane back to the carrier with one strand of wire holding one rudder control and with the other rudder completely shot away. One pilot who was relatively new with the fleet crashed on his initial take-off in the dark because there was no horizon that morning and he did not have the experience to fly off into nothing without some bearing.

These stories made us realize that Americans were actually fighting in the Pacific, and they whetted our zeal in training. I think that at that time we were all anxious to get into the scrap. To pilots the advice of the side liners to "go get those dirty bastards" lacks an understanding of the real grimness of war.

2

Check-Out Aboard U.S.S. "Hornet"

A LARGE CARRIER in our fleet constitutes one of the most compact and deadly striking forces on land or sea today. Carrying seventy or more of the best fighting planes of their types available in the world, the American carrier is designed to pursue a purely offensive war. The ship and her crew live for the day of the swift and annihilating attack—the sudden and fierce stab at the vitals of the enemy. A secret approach by sea to within aircraft range of the objective, an undiscovered flight to the target, and a hasty withdrawal form the ideal of this vicious blow.

To this purpose the aircraft aboard are divided, in general, into three types: fighters, scout dive bombers, and torpedo planes. Usually there are four squadrons aboard, each a separate unit, yet each operating in conjunction with the others.

The primary mission of the fighters is to destroy enemy aircraft, either those attempting to prevent our dive bombers and torpedo planes from carrying out their attacks successfully or enemy bombers and torpedo planes attacking our carrier. While the carrier is heading toward its objective fighters on "combat patrol" constantly hover over the mother ship on guard against a surprise thrust by land-based bombers or planes from another flat-top. This is boring duty for the pilot, who must flutter around at 100 knots at high altitude, wearing an oxygen mask, saving gas, and waiting—waiting for a crack at the Japs. A fighter can stay in the air anywhere from two to five hours, depending on whether the pilot hoards his supply of gas by flying at slow speed or opens the throttle when he gets in a scrap and eats up the octane power available.

When the big day comes and the carrier launches its attack this combat patrol is augmented. The remainder of the fighters either take off to protect the attack group or stand by with engines warmed to launch at the first sign of enemy planes in the vicinity.

Carrier-based fighters accompanying the attack groups have also been used to drop light 100-pound bombs and to strafe planes on the ground, personnel, A.A. positions, and ships. There is on record more than one sinking of Jap destroyers by strafing fighters alone.

The standard fighter in the fleet in those days was the F4F (the Grumman Wildcat), a little beer bottle of a plane with a battery of .50-caliber guns in its tiny wings. Again and again it has proven itself the equal of the vaunted Zero if employed with the correct tactics. Its successor, the F6F (the Grumman Hell-cat), is a more powerful aircraft and is now on its way to the fleet. The first squadrons to fly the F4U (the Corsair), a big, new, sleek-looking fighter with a queer, inverted gull wing, are operating with the fleet now.

There are two squadrons of dive bombers on a large carrier. One is dubbed a scouting squadron and the other a bombing squadron, but they are used interchangeably for both jobs. Each day at dawn and every afternoon the dive bombers whine up the deck and leave the ship to scout miles ahead of and around the force, searching for any evidence of a hostile presence. They are the "eyes of the ship," and it is upon their radioed reports that the strategy of attack is based.

On the offensive the dive bombers tuck 500-pound or 1,000-pound "eggs" behind their props and launch to "hawk 'em." The SBD has been the work horse dive bomber of our Navy since the war began. Now the SB2C, the Helldiver, a bigger, faster plane capable of carrying heavier bombs and packing more gun power, is going into the active war zone.

The fourth squadron aboard is the torpedo squadron. The pilot of a torpedo bomber has one objective fixed in his mind. He must take the big, ungainly weapon charged with TNT that he is carrying on his plane's underside to within several hundred yards of an enemy ship and drop it in such a position that it will run a straight course, intercept the vessel, and sink it. There are other uses for the plane—horizontal bombing from altitude, glide bombing, and searching, for example—but it was built primarily to carry a torpedo to a place where it will do some good. Up until Midway the TBD (Douglas Devastator) was our Navy's torpedo carrier. After this plane was shot into oblivion in that engagement it was replaced by the TBF (Grumman Avenger).

The maximum striking power of the carrier is put into play when the fighters, dive bombers, and torpedo planes are used in conjunction in a well-timed, fully co-ordinated attack. When this is done the blows delivered by each of the individual units carry more sting, and, moreover, each unit affords the other mutual protection from opposition encountered. The tactics vary, but a good one-two-three punch on an enemy vessel might have the dive bombers pouring down from altitude first, followed by strafing fighters, if there were no enemy fighters, with the torpedo planes throwing their fish in the water just as the fighters were pulling up. In this way the decks are cleared of A.A. gunners as the torpedo planes get within vulnerable range and they are allowed to drop before being shot down.

The flight deck of a carrier is so small in comparison to an average landing field that flight operations aboard must be timed to the split second and to the inch. Before take-off all aircraft are spotted on the other half of the deck, the fighters in front, the dive bombers behind them, and the torpedo planes on the stern. The planes are stacked so closely together that sometimes there is not six inches between a propeller blade whipping the air at 1,500 revolutions per minute and the delicate fabric of the tail surfaces on the plane ahead. Wings are folded to allow as many planes on deck as possible at one time.

When the carrier turns into the wind and the fly one officer gets the nod from the air officer in his "box" above on the island structure the first fighter in "the spot" gets ready for take-off. As fly one agitates his take-off wand in the right hand the pilot revs his engine up to full power with the brakes still applied, gives thumbs up to indicate plane okay, then lets go of the brakes and lumbers up the deck when fly one points toward the bow. The next plane is in the spot with wings spread ready to go as the first is rising off the bow. Gradually the deck is cleared, and if there are any more planes to go they are shot up from the hangar deck on large elevators, already "turning up."

When the planes come home again and it is time to land them, the carrier wheels into the wind and the signal officer takes his position. There are several arresting wires on the deck, and the hook on the pilot's plane may catch any one of them. If the plane catches the first wire near the stern it is brought to a gradual stop with plenty of slack wire unraveling to ease the jolt. The tension on the wires increases as it nears the barrier, and catching the last wire jerks the plane like a dog at the end of a rope. A crash into the barrier is not as serious as it sounds. It's about like hitting a brick wall in a car going forty miles an hour, and the pilot, who is strapped in by his safety belt, usually takes only a black eye or a split lip down to the ready room with him.

The fighter pilot is a lone shark. He flies by himself, he gets angry by himself, and he talks to himself, if anybody. But two and three men share the sensations of flight and combat in a dive bomber and torpedo plane respectively.

Perhaps a dive bomber pilot and his radioman-gunner—the latter sits behind the pilot facing aft nursing his guns and gazing over the tail at the sky—become more friendly than do the crew of the torpedo plane: the two of them are together up there under the sun and the paleness of the blue sky, and they feel a bond. They swap jokes during long search flights, they tell each other about their girls at home, and sometimes they even sing songs over the interphone. Jamie said his radioman always used to yodel the popular song "I don't want to set the world on fire, I just want to make love," whenever they started out on a dangerous bombing mission. If they are together long enough, and a pilot carries the same crew on every trip, they are bound to know each other well after a few hops.

Before we could join the teams of these fighting planes as

pilots in the operating squadrons of the fleet we had to prove that we could land on a carrier deck; we had to qualify. For some time we had been awaiting the opportunity.

The U.S.S. *Hornet*, one of the Navy's newest aircraft carriers, hove in sight on Friday, March 20, and docked a few hours later. Her lopsided structure was visible far out toward the horizon, and as she sailed into the foreground and passed through the channel she looked like a monstrous perversion.

On Saturday the pilots in the Red and Blue Squadrons were given the word to check out of the advanced carrier training group and board the carrier for a short cruise to qualify in carrier landings. For many weeks we had been simulating carrier landings on a stationary field under the painstaking instruction of Lieutenant Ray Needham, who acted as signal officer. Now we were to try our hand at landing on the deck of a ship under way.

Mr. Needham had taken such an interest in hammering at the individual faults of each student, one by one, that when they returned a year later he could tell any one of them what his mistakes had been. One continually "overshot the groove"—he needed more right rudder; another had a tendency to "rise at the ramp"—he was too fast; and a third would not respond to a "high dip" with the paddles. Mr. Needham had by a variety of methods ironed out these errors one after another. At times during field carrier landing practice he would stand in the signal officer's box waving signal after signal at an approaching plane, coaxing the pilot into position for a landing. He seemed almost to be flying the plane himself. "He's a few knots too fast," you would hear him remark, or "Pick that wing up," or, "Nose up—nose up—nose up," as the plane came up the groove. Again, after indicating to a student that he was making the same mistake on each approach in every way that he could from the ground, Ray would drop the paddles in a pretense of giving up and just stand there with a disgusted look on his face as the plane roared by. This usually started the pilot thinking for himself. If he got irritated enough Needham would throw the paddles at the plane as it passed. These tactics were effective. So was the psychology he applied on the ground in talking to the students. He always smiled when he spoke to them, and the main idea he tried to put over was, "You can do it. Here's how."

We packed and boarded the *Hornet*, which we soon came to know as the "Horny Maru," on Monday, March 23. It was the first time many of us had been to sea on a U.S. warship, and we were as green to the ways of the Navy as the dumbest boot. The procedure on going aboard is to salute the ensign aft (a flag, not an officer) and then to salute the officer of the deck and ask permission to come aboard. Although we had been taught navy traditions in school we had forgotten most of them, and we made all the mistakes in the book. Many of us, including myself, saluted forward instead of aft, and I heard one polite but hardly military request to the officer of the deck from an ensign who beseeched, "May I please come aboard your boat, sir?"

Once on the quarter-deck, we wandered around bumping into busy seamen whom we envied for knowing what they were about and tripping over mooring lines until we were instructed to report to the captain's quarters with our orders. From there we were sent to the first lieutenant's office to get room assignments, and I was surprised to find that the first lieutenant was a lieutenant commander. It was very confusing. Somehow I thought he should be a lieutenant.

For the remainder of the cruise we made blunders. We got lost—"Which way is the dining room?" we would ask of some sailor. "The wardroom is on the first deck amidships," he would answer, and we wouldn't know any more than before. We fell down and tripped over coamings, we got seasick, we were halted by a Marine sentry as we were just about to enter the captain's country, and we barked our shins on steel ladders until they were black and blue.

The "Horny Maru" weighed anchor and the tugs pulled her into the channel about 10:30 in the morning. She put to sea, accompanied by her destroyer guard, on a course southwest. Soon we were out of sight of land without being aware of it. We spent all the time possible topside, where the smell of the fresh salt air and the play of the buffeting wind across the unguarded flight deck exhilarated us. The great bull horns or loudspeakers on the island continually were blasting forth orders and announcements with bugle calls and the ridiculous scream of the bos'n's whistle. There was always noise on the carrier deck—the ripping of the wind in the rigging on the island structure, the wash of the water alongside, and the pounding of the great ship in the sea, if nothing else—but these sounds tended to create peace rather than confusion. The smoke drifting from the stacks was cleared by the wind almost immediately and wasn't unpleasant.

"This is great stuff," Dick Jaccard said. "Katharine Hepburn would cut quite a figure standing on the bridge, hair streaming in the wind and eyes lifted to eternity."

Dick, Jamie, and I, along with the others, went below to the wardroom for "chow" shortly after noon and were surprised at the high quality of food and service. The wardroom, or the officer's messroom, was a well-lighted saloon with a low ceiling which ran the breadth of the ship. We were seated at long tables covered with silky linen—the senior officers, those above the rank of lieutenant (jg), at a special table of their own—and were served tastefully prepared dishes by colored mess attendants who seemed ready to jump to your elbow at every moment. The *Hornet* had its own monogrammed silver.

The food on carriers is generally quite good for the first month after stocking up and putting to sea. Thereafter it begins to deteriorate. Fresh milk disappears almost immediately, and the next to go are fresh eggs, greens and fresh vegetables, and finally fresh meat. Officers and crew alike begin to live on powdered milk, powdered eggs, and canned fruit and vegetables and meat. The mess treasurer can always manage to stir up a good meal before and after an engagement, however, to give the morale of the pilots a shot in the arm.

After luncheon we went topside again and assembled in the fighters' ready room to get a last-minute pep talk by Mr. Needham before beginning our qualifications.

Each combat squadron aboard an aircraft carrier has its own ready room where the pilots spend most of their time during the day going through drills in navigation, radio code, and recognition of enemy ships and planes, discussing tactics or playing cards. It is their headquarters on the ship, and they literally live and sleep there when they are not in their own quarters. The gunners, radiomen, and bombardiers who man the dive bombers and torpedo planes are brought into their ready room for special sessions from time to time, but usually they are busied with their squadron duties on the hangar deck below.

Since this was only a training cruise and there were no regular squadrons aboard, we had been assigned the VF, or fighters' briefing room. Needham told us all that there was nothing to making carrier landings, as we had expected he would, and we didn't believe him, as he expected we wouldn't. I think he preferred to have us a little nervous so we would be on our toes.

The dive bombers began to qualify about two o'clock in the afternoon. Eight planes were available. The sea was not rough, but the swell was mean and the wind high. The ship was pitching considerably, so that at the ramp—the stern of the flight deck—there was as much as thirty feet variation. Three of the dive bombers we sent below when their engines cut out at high r.p.m.—"because," said Mr. Needham, "the pilots didn't keep them revved up enough before take-off and the plugs fouled." Five finally rumbled down the deck and took off safely with plenty of lift to spare.

Mr. Needham took his post on the signal officer's platform aft on the portside and prepared to take them aboard. The signal officer operates with a pair of circular paddles which resemble tennis rackets. The circular part is usually covered with red bunting in the daytime, since this is the color most easily distinguished under normal lighting conditions. The left-hand paddle has a long handle, which the signal officer lays along his arm, but the right-hand paddle has a shorter stem, which is more maneuverable.

By holding these two paddles in different positions the signal officer indicates to the pilot what changes to make in the attitude of the plane and in the pattern of approach in order to be in position to land. An "R," or "Roger," made by holding both paddles horizontally out from the body, means the approach is correct. When both paddles are held overhead the pilot knows he is too high; when they are both 45° down from the horizontal he is too low. With the right-hand paddle 45° down and the left horizontal the plane is too fast. If the signal officer moves his paddles together in front of his body and then rows backward with them the plane is too slow. When the plane is in the proper position astern of the ramp the signal officer gives the pilot a "cut" by chopping his right hand across his throat and the pilot closes his throttle and makes his landing. A "wave-off," made by crisscrossing the paddles overhead, is signaled when the plane in the groove is in an impossible or dangerous position to land. There are other signals, but these are the principal ones.

Those who were not flying climbed up on the island structure and went aft to watch the landings. I believe that a carrier landing is the most thrilling action sight there is in peacetime. It is much more spectacular than horse racing or auto racing or boxing, although it compares with ski jumping. To take a fast plane, heavy with armor plate, machine guns, gas, and sometimes bombs, and set it down on a short, narrow deck requires all the attention and skill of the most experienced pilot. When the pilots have never done it before and are nervous, to say the least, it is that much more spectacular.

Ensign Edmondson made the first landing, a good one squarely in the center of the deck. Then Lieutenant (jg) Paul Holmberg came up the groove, took the cut, and landed to the portside of the deck. The wire caught his hook and threw his tail outboard, dragging his left wheel within a foot of the edge of the deck. That was the first hint we who were watching the operations had that there might be some trouble.

From that point things began to happen fast.

Coming in for his next landing, Edmondson gets a cut but holds the plane off too long and comes floating up the deck kept in the air somehow, although it seems impossible. The ship alarm horn is blaring in his face as he crashes head on into the island structure and the first wire barrier. He is not hurt, but the bent prop looks like the petals on a flower, and his right wing is crumpled. The undercarriage is not smashed, and the deck handlers disentangle him. We watch them push him up the deck sitting in his plane looking white and disappointed.

Ensign Goddard has the next crash. After the cut he lands too far to starboard, and when the wire catches the hook it tosses the plane and throws his right wheel and wing off the deck and into the banks of A.A. guns. His wheel shaft is broken and the wing crumpled.

The fighters take over when there are only three dive bombers left. The Wildcat pilots make good landings for a while, and then the most exciting crash of the afternoon occurs.

Ensign Dibb, flying an F4F, takes the cut, hits wheels first just forward of the ramp, bounces once again, and then crashes squarely into the wire barrier with the plane still in flight and afire. The gas valve under the plane has been knocked off, and a bright blanket of flame shoots from the nose over the belly of the plane as it noses up. Dibb literally dives out of the cockpit, hits the wing with his shoulder, and rolls off onto the deck. He falls almost into the arms of two asbestos-suited men, the "Asbestos Joes," who are running to his aid. He is unhurt, but they hurry him away to sick bay to see the doctor as the fire crews rush to deal with the blaze.

The fire crews open up first with CO_2 bottles and then with hoses, squirting a soda preparation on the burning plane. The fire is not extensive yet, and everyone thinks it will soon be put out. Then pressure on the hoses fails, and immediately the plane begins to burn fiercely again. The carrier deck itself catches fire. The plane cracks and buckles under the heat. One of the gas tanks bursts a hole in the fuselage of the plane and shoots a stream of fuel into the fire. The cockpit shield reaches combustible point and torches up. The carrier is afire now, and fire call has been sounded.

At the critical moment pressure is obtained on the hoses again, and the fire crews struggling with the blaze soon succeed in drowning the burning area in a flood of white soda. They put the fire out completely, and the two grotesque parts of the plane which remain are hauled below.

When the qualifications were over for the day and we had

had dinner we retired to our quarters in officers' country in the forward part of the ship two or three decks down from the flight deck to discuss carrier landings all over again. The officers live in small staterooms, one or two to a room. Mess attendants clean the rooms, make the beds, change the linen and towels, and shine shoes left outside the doors. If there is more than one bunk in a room they are stacked, shipshape, one above the other. It was into these neat, compact quarters that groups of us crowded that night to hash and rehash the day's landings and to think about our landings on the morrow.

The next morning the fighters begin qualifying again. Ensign Kleinman, making the second take-off, roars up the deck and disappears off the starboard bow. Splash—his plane has hit the water. He forgot to crack his flaps. In a moment we see him aside his plane, his life jacket inflated, waving to us that he is okay and then splashing backward with his hands to clear his sinking plane. We watch as his plane, nose down, and he drift aft, both getting smaller and smaller. The trailing destroyer changes course to pick him up. He is out of sight now, and only the tail of his plane is visible. It sinks. In a few moments, however, the destroyer signals by blinker "Have pilot," and the fact of the rescue is announced over the loud-speaker.

A sailor who has seen carrier qualifications before is standing next to me, and he tells us that we aren't doing badly and that usually there are more accidents when new pilots attempt landings. We think he is exaggerating, but nevertheless it makes us all a little fidgety. We have seen both fire and water hazards now and are yet to qualify.

As we watch, Ensign Eppler takes the cut, hits the deck to starboard, and catches a wire. But his plane goes over the side, hanging there a moment until his hook slips from the wire, and then it disappears from our sight beneath the flange of the deck. Soon he appears astern, bobbing in the water. His plane is just sinking. He too is picked up by the destroyer.

"Only two more, and they'll have enough for bridge over there," cracks Durkin.

The weather is squally and the swells high as the SBDs

start to qualify again. When my turn comes and I hop into the cockpit I am nervous but eager for the experience. Just before I go out Mr. Needham tells us that most of us are too high and too fast. As I am making my first approach I think of this and consequently go to the other extreme. I am low and slow. Needham rows me in, gives me a wave-off, and then falls flat on the deck as I hurtle over not five feet above the ramp. On the next trip I get a cut and land and am surprised at the tug of the wire, which I had forgotten about. But I am aboard and the tension is over. I remember that I was able to see the carrier deck at the cut—which somebody told me I wouldn't—and am relieved at that. I make my next three landings without a wave-off and am qualified.

Later, in the ready room, Mr. Needham came up to me and showed me his thumb, which he had strained getting out of the way of my plane on my first approach. Then he grinned and said, "Well, I guess we made a Christian out of you after that."

Being aboard a carrier for the first time is a strange experience. On the flat flight deck the wind is always clean and strong and the view across to the sea uncluttered by ship's gear. The water is fresh with whitecaps, and astern the destroyer slices through the sea, ever graceful and ever attendant.

During operations the flight deck crew, wearing helmets of different colors according to their duties, are on the deck crouching against the wind and the slip stream from the planes' propellers. They look like monkeys or men from a different world. They scamper from the sides when a plane lands in order to unhook the wire or swarm all over the crash scene in case of an accident. They are all over the deck and always moving quickly.

The carrier at dusk is at its strangest and most beautiful. An hour before sunset the call to general quarters sounds, and all hands lay to their stations. The ship is blacked out, the hatches are closed, and quiet falls about the vessel as the sun goes down.

Below on the hangar deck the only lights are dim colored ones—red, green, and midnight blue. All is gloom and quiet except for sudden unidentified shadows and sounds. Small knots of men talk in low voices. An oil pan scrapes across the deck as it is moved. A flicker marks a sailor groping his way down through the planes with the aid of a pin-point flashlight. The hangar elevator falls away, and the dusk light breaks through. A short sharp whistle from the chief directing operations, and it shoots up again.

Above on the flight deck the men stand at their gun stations watching the sun sink to the westward and the faint light of early stars come into the sky. During this hallowed hour they talk in softer voices, if at all, and think of the things their mothers believe are always in their minds.

3

Into the War Zone

WHEN WE RETURNED from four days aboard the *Hornet* we were given instructions to report to new duty in four days.

"It's going to be awfully drunk out the next few days," Jim Shelton said, and he was right.

I don't know why we drank so much during our last few hours in Coronado, but I suppose we found that it made it easier to express our excitement at going, to show our friendliness for one another, and to think of things to say to those we were leaving.

On the last night Jamie Dexter and his girl tried to drink a pint of 150-proof Demerara rum apiece; Bill Pittman went to see Little Natalie; Harry Frederickson called on each of his girls and their mothers, allotting every household a half-hour of his time; and Jim Shelton and I sat in our favorite bar and talked about what we thought was going to happen.

When it came time to leave we packed our carefully inventoried belongings and our hang-overs into Jamie's car and drove up the coast. There we found an anticlimax awaiting us in the form of a two-day delay before we sailed on the transport which was to take us into the war zone. However, we forced ourselves to see the town before we left. With a few stimulants, all of us were in good form again. Jamie, Jim Shelton, Bill Pittman, and I breezed through all our money on the last night and were preparing to go back to the ship, writing a check for the cab. On the

45

way back Pittman found an overlooked dollar bill in his pocket, and this we tore in four parts—one for each of us— and put into our wallets for good-luck pieces. These talismans were not very effective. Only two of us saw the States again.

The transport sailed out of the harbor the next morning (April 8), on a beautiful spring day. The ship sloughed her moorings at about 9:30 o'clock, and tugs nosed her out into the stream. There we could see the other transports of the convoy and a number of warships—American battle wagons, cruisers, and tin cans. We steamed down the bay.

We were leaving a beautiful city, clean and sparkling and green, as we saw it from the bay that morning. The skyscrapers were strung all over the hills on the south side, and they were shining in the sun as we headed out to sea. The verdure of the hills and the many indentures in the harbor took away the smoky, organized aspect of the large city and left an impression fresh and golden.

Out of the harbor and into the seaward channel our convoy rode with a destroyer on either side. The sea gulls wheeled and croaked noisily about the stern; the wash of the bow wave and the hiss of the salt steadied into a familiar pattern. We passed buoy after buoy, some rocking a slow and melancholy bell and others moaning with an unearthly warning as if from the caves of the sea. We sighted sharks astern, but they refused to follow us.

The coast became an outline, and we were swallowed in the sameness and solitude of the ocean. As the ship labored through the long swells in a fresh sea, the mosaic of noises reached a pattern without rhythm or definite interval yet establishing a slow, sad, and tedious tempo. Life on deck seemed a series of creaks, grindings, moans, whirs, and flappings. The vessel rose and fell, rolled and listed and yawed, wind moaned through the shroud lines and halyards, canvas tarpaulins beat against their moorings, and a thousand bangings and scrapings came from all quarters. Underrunning all this was the steady thrum of the engines in the bowels of the ship as they drove the great screws that bit into the sea.

Jamie and I were assigned the port and starboard skyline

watches on the poop deck and went to our stations as soon as we had cleared the channel. As we searched the sky for enemy planes that we never expected to sight we began to enjoy again the strange simplicity of the sea. We watched the salt patterns dissolve and remake themselves in the boiling wake astern, and we felt the sting of the spindrift while smoking cigarettes and settling into that calm of mind which the ocean brings. Once we saw a whale, first catching him by his wheezing spray and later making out his dark form on the water.

The danger from enemy attack, especially by submarine, was always present, but apparently existence was peaceful and we were so little used to being in the war zone that this threat disturbed us only slightly. On the fourth day out discipline relaxed somewhat. We were no longer required to wear life jackets except on duty. All we had to do besides standing a four hours' watch every sixteen hours was eat and sleep, read and talk. The temperature rose, and the warm sky and healthy breeze made life easy and pleasant.

In the quiet life aboard ship I got to know my friends better than I had before. Jamie was an outright romanticist, I discovered, who thought of the war as a great adventure. Standing the watch on the poop deck, he would relate for me the sensations he expected to go through in battle or tell me his plans for after the war. He wanted to go to South America, he said, because he thought there would be opportunities there and because it appealed to him to exploit a new frontier. Jamie read books like *John Paul Jones* and *The Sun is My Undoing* and *Anthony Adverse,* and in his diary he expressed himself in an old-fashioned way: "... on this fourteenth day of April, year of our Lord," etc. Sometimes, I think, he even thought of himself as a sort of Anthony Adverse. He didn't have many of the qualities of an Anthony, though, for he was too kindhearted and his sense of humor was too fine.

I think Jamie aspired to a sort of squire's life. He liked the social sports, tennis, swimming, and skiing, and I believe he thought something of "background." At cocktail parties he was always polite to the hostess and the mothers and helped them mix cocktails in the kitchen and pass them to the guests. He treated all women in a gentlemanly, almost chivalrous manner—even some of the old hags we used to run into. The younger girls of Coronado thought of him as the perfect husband.

This was not a shallow thing with Jamie, however. He was very considerate of his mother, too. Some gentle thing within him, not his head, told him to be the way he was. This is not to imply that Jamie was a fool. He had a good head about practical things and carried his ideas out with a great deal of energy.

He was not a sad-faced romanticist either. He was a gay one. It was usually he who noticed that the cocktail hour was approaching and who wanted to go "down to the La Fiesta for a nightcap" on Mondays.

In Dick Jaccard there was a lot of the romanticist, too, but he affected a cynicism which was both healthy and gay. He usually was the loudest in laughing down any conceited or pompous statement, and he was very sensitive to any phony appeals to our patriotism. He was good-looking in an open, fair-haired way, and the movements of his body were lithe and graceful. I used to call him "the Falcon," which is what he reminded me of with his flight helmet on. Others called him "Jake the Rake" or "Monsieur Jaccard." On the surface Dick was always lighthearted, with a ready wit and an infectious laugh. Several times, though, I saw him with his face in repose, and then the corners of his mouth were turned way down.

There was something of a fundamental, philosophical nature that was bothering Jaccard, but he never let anyone know what it was. Perhaps he didn't know himself. At any rate, he usually was able to mask any personal doubts of his own in an apparently spontaneous good humor which was very refreshing. He had a quick mind, a hearty laugh, and an engaging enthusiasm. I liked him because he always was willing to do anything that sounded as though it might have some excitement connected with it.

Jim Shelton was perhaps the most truly generous person I have known. He would lend anybody money if he had it, and he was always willing to stand a watch for a friend. He never tried to be the smartest person in a conversation. His whole spirit seemed to enjoy doing things for others.

There were ten nurses aboard, but although one or two were good-looking nobody except the ship's officers paid much attention to them. In our minds, we had left all such nonsense behind and were bound for adventures which had more to offer than the touché and riposte of sex. The ebb and flow of one particular romance interested us from an objective point of view, but I'm afraid we took a rather tolerant and superior attitude toward it.

Early on the ninth day (Thursday, April 17) we sighted the island of Molokai, in the Hawaiian group, and turned south to pass between Molokai and Oahu. Everybody was on deck, jammed forward to see what they could, as we approached closer and closer to the islands. There was some difficulty in determining which promontory was Diamond Head. We had heard that it was the first piece of land visible, but it distinctly is not, at least on an approach from the north.

The ship entered Pearl Harbor through an opening in the submarine net, and we stood waiting to become aghast at the scene of wholesale destruction we were sure would greet us. But four and one half months after December 7 the damage from the Jap attack seemed relatively slight compared to what rumors had us believing.

Nevertheless, all evidence of the treachery had not been erased. A thick oil film at least two feet deep rimmed the entire bay. Large steel masts which had been removed from one of the sunken battleships were lying on the bank in the channel entrance. As we passed Ford Island, in the center of the bay, we saw the rusted hull of the overturned *Oklahoma* and, in a line with her bulk, the turrets of the *California* just awash. The buckled and twisted mass of steel which had been the *Arizona* lay beyond the *California*. On the other side of Ford Island was the target ship *Utah* keel skyward. One or two of the hangars on Ford Island were mere skeletons.

Otherwise all the havoc done by the Japs had been repaired. I was surprised too at the smallness of Pearl Harbor. Because it was so important I had conceived of it as comparing with large anchorages, like Norfolk and San Francisco, in the United States. Perhaps because the harbor is set so unostentatiously amidst the expanse of green fields on the island with the mountains towering beyond, its size is dwarfed.

Hawaii, or rather Oahu, on the other hand, lived up to my conception of it. The high mountains blanketed with green, the sloping plantation lands covered with sugar cane and pineapple, the warm sun and the brilliantly covered sea and fine-grained sandy beaches were all there.

Once ashore on Oahu, we crossed to Ford Island and reported to Comairbatfor (Commander Aircraft Battle Force), who assigned us to our squadrons. Nine among us had been given ground training as torpedo plane pilots, and we were sent on temporary duty to Torpedo Squadron Three. The next day we drove over the Pali to the windward side of the island, where the Kaneohe Naval Air Station is situated, and reported to the squadron's skipper, Lieutenant Commander Massey. We were supposed to be the first new torpedo plane pilots to reach the fleet since the war started.

John Armitage, Bob Divine, and I had original orders to Torpedo Squadron Two, aboard the *Lexington*, and expected to be transferred in order to join this unit soon.

Not a week after we had reported to Torpedo Three, Jamie Dexter, Tom Durkin, Dick Jaccard, and Ensign Vammen were reassigned to a scouting squadron and a few days later slipped out to sea on a carrier. Just as suddenly Harry Frederickson left to board a transport which was to take him to a scouting squadron on another carrier in the South Pacific.

Those of us who remained in Torpedo Three began training in the TBD (the Douglas Devastator), the torpedo plane which carried the burden of the fight at Midway. This craft was far ahead of its time when it first made its appearance in the fleet during the middle thirties. It is a sturdy, stable plane with exceptionally clean lines. But in comparison with opposing aircraft at the beginning of the war, it was far outclassed. It is underpowered, extremely slow and unmaneuverable, and no match for the Zero. Even so, at the time it compared favorably with other torpedo planes in use, both Allied and Axis.

During our training we flew this plane with and without torpedoes, in the daytime and at night. We made horizontal bombing runs and simulated torpedo attacks. We trained the gunners by sailing past a sleeve while they blistered it with holes. We prepared ourselves to land on a carrier with innumerable sessions of "bounce drill."

On one of our training hops the squadron flew to the island of Maui, which is reputed to be the most beautiful of all the Hawaiians. To me it seemed neither more nor less a garden spot than the other islands. On the trip to Maui we flew close along the coast of Molokai. Fifteen-hundred-foot cliffs falling straight into the sea were shrouded in rain clouds on top, and long, lacy fingers of waterfall streaked down the sides of the rock as in a fairyland.

The brilliant coloring and the proximity of sea and land are what make all the islands beautiful and give them their appearance of unreality. The bright red coral earth, the pastels of the sea, the pure white strands of beach, and the purple shadows formed in mountain, cloud, and water are arresting. There is something peculiarly exhilarating too in the air about Hawaii, which combines the promise of spring with the tang of autumn. The heat is not overpowering. When it gets hot it gets cloudy, and the clouds hide the sun, or it rains.

One aspect of flying around Hawaii that I noticed was the rough air. It was the bumpiest I've ever encountered. Rounding Diamond Head on the trip from Kaneohe on the windward side of Oahu to Ford Island, the plane would be tossed up and down like a leaf, sometimes dropping as much as one hundred feet.

One day the squadron took part in a combined practice attack on a destroyer southwest of Pearl Harbor. Fighters were to escort the dive bombers to the push-over point, and we were to come in fanned out on the bows as a separate group just as the dive bombers completed their attack.

As I was heading in to drop my exercise fish I saw an explosion of water to my starboard. It was one of the dive bombers hitting the sea. A fighter had collided with the bomber in midair and ripped a wing from the latter. The fighter was relatively undamaged and returned to the base, but the bomber spun in. The pilot of the bomber was able to bail out, and the radioman-gunner in the second cockpit, who couldn't get out, was killed. The pilot did the only reasonable thing when he abandoned a ship out of control and saved his own life, but somehow there is always a shadow of blame cast on an airman who bails out and leaves his crew to their fate—at least until the investigation clears him. In this case—and this is the point of the tale—at the funeral of the radioman the chaplain had the poor taste to choose as his text a theme which made us all wince—the last lines of Tennyson's poem "Crossing the Bar," which run:

> I hope to meet my Pilot face to face
> When I have crossed the bar.

A new type of officer joined the aircraft squadrons when we were in Hawaii. He was the A-V(S), or aircraft specialist. These officers were all men who had had extensive executive experience and had been trained in a hurry-up course at Quonset, Rhode Island, to assume administrative duties in the squadrons of the fleet. I believe there was a minor upheaval when they were first introduced to the operating units. At the extremes, they regarded themselves as the brains and the fliers as the brawn of the squadrons; on the other hand, the fliers, especially the older ones, looked upon them as apprentice paper boys. The trouble soon ironed out, however, when they proved themselves capable, intelligent, and useful and cast off the veneer of Naval Tradition they had acquired and became human again.

About the 10th of May news of the Coral Sea engagement became definite enough to establish a victory for the Allies. At the same time disturbing rumors that the *Lexington* had been sunk began to seep through, and they became stronger as the month progressed. We who were assigned to her began to wonder if we would ever go aboard.

I was on the second day of my fortnightly liberty in Honolulu when I heard from another officer that the carrier Jamie had sailed on had returned to Pearl Harbor. I immediately began to look for my friends and finally found them in various stages of hilarity and hang-over at the Moana Hotel, near Waikiki Beach.

Jim Shelton was groaning in the bed, Vammen was calling up some girl he had met the night before, and Jamie was hunting for his clothes. Jaccard took a flower out of a water glass and invited me to have a drink.

They all looked quite thin after only a month out. They had been down in the Coral Sea but had not taken part in the battle.

Tom Durkin was missing. He had become lost on a single-plane search mission, and the last anybody heard from him was his radio call that he was making a water landing. Jamie thought he would have a good chance of surviving if he landed safely and got into his rubber boat, because there were many islands in the vicinity.

The *Lexington* definitely had been sunk, the boys said. This news meant that I probably would join Torpedo Three permanently.

But it turned out differently. When I returned to the Royal Hawaiian that afternoon I found a note instructing me to report back to the base immediately. I caught a taxi, drove back over the Pali to Kaneohe, and hurried to squadron headquarters. There I was told I had a half-hour to pack my personal gear and catch a truck for Ford Island for temporary duty with Torpedo Squadron Eight. Bob Divine and Rudy Karzmar, a regular member of Torpedo Two who had been sick and then been transferred to Torpedo Three, were to go with me.

At Ford Island we reported to Lieutenant Commander John C. Waldron, the lean, fierce-looking skipper of our new squadron. When he found out that Divine and I had never landed on a carrier in a TBD he did not want us at first but finally consented to take us as spare pilots.

That night I boarded the "Horny Maru" for the second time, but this time I was sure that our purpose was not to qualify green pilots.

4

Torpedo Squadron Eight

To CLEAR UP ANY MISUNDERSTANDING which might arise because activities of Torpedo Eight have been chronicled as taking place after the Midway battle, in which the entire squadron is supposed to have been wiped out, it would be well to explain that there were two divisions of the squadron. Originally, when the unit was organized in the fall of 1941, both were together as one group in Norfolk, Virginia, under command of Waldron. This group split in February 1942, and one division went to sea with Waldron on the *Hornet* while the other stayed in Norfolk to train in the new TBFs under command of Larsen. Larsen's detachment reached Pearl Harbor just before the Midway battle, and six of his planes were sent out to the island.

We sailed aboard the *Hornet* from Pearl Harbor as part of a task force. I went on the flight deck after lunch, when we were in the open sea, and was amazed at the size of our force and at the way the cruisers and destroyers were boiling around the sea in all directions about us. The *Hornet* itself wheeled sharply once or twice, and the flat surface of the flight deck made a crazy angle with the horizon.

The first announcement of our mission was made over the loud-speaker system to all hands in the afternoon. Practically all that was said was, "We are going out to intercept a Jap attack on Midway." Period. But a friend whom I had known at school, Ensign Charles McCormick, then a deck officer on the *Hornet*, thought that the Japs recently had been concentrating for a thrust at the Aleutians or Hawaiians. Activity in the Coral Sea recently could have been designed to divert our forces to the south. The first stage of an attack on the Hawaiians might be to feint at Oahu with bombers in order to suck in our defense, McCormick thought, followed by an attempt to seize Midway.

The planes from our ship and from the other carrier in our task force flew out to come aboard the first day, and the sky seemed to be filled with them. All got aboard safely, except one torpedo plane, which we saw go over the side of the other carrier.

After our skipper, Commander Waldron, came aboard, we spent most of our time in the ready room, where he mapped out the possible course of the approaching battle for us and prepared his already superbly trained pilots for what lay ahead. Day by day the nature of our mission unfolded, and Waldron interpreted it to us. We crept nearer and nearer to the battle.

The boys in that ready room came from all parts of the country and from all classes of society. They formed a typical cross section of young America. But they were not average young Americans by any means. Each seemed to have his own special talent and gift of personality.

They were knit together as a unit, almost as a family, by the long hours of training under their skipper. They all knew each other well. It seemed to me they treated Divine, Karzmar, and me as a large family would treat outsiders. They were friendly and polite to us, as a family group would be to visitors, but among themselves they bickered and bantered as though they had been together for years.

Waldron gave to the squadron that special character of aggressiveness and earnestness in training which so distinguished it from other squadrons of the fleet. The motto of these torpedomen was "Attack"—that and nothing more— and the squadron insignia, a closed fist. The purpose of the squadron was that simple, as conceived by Waldron. We were at war, and there was only one thing for an aircraft squadron to do, and that was to fight, to strike, to "attack," not once, but again and again.

Everything Waldron did was toward the one aim of

preparing the pilots for this purpose. In training at Norfolk, he flew them six to eight hours a day. He mdae them learn things about their planes that pilots had never learned before—how to make engine changes, how to take off a flipper and set a new one, how to load a torpedo, and how the hydraulic system worked. He gave lecture after lecture on torpedo plane tactics and explained to his pilots how a well-planned and firmly executed attack could not fail to drive home several fish.

Then about the time the boys began to say, "Oh, to hell with it," and think there couldn't be any sense to working so hard, Waldron threw a big party for them at his home. They all brought their girls, and everyone had plenty to eat and drink. It was almost like New Year's Eve every time this happened. They danced, they got down on their knees and shot craps, they argued and bellowed at each other, and they rolled on the floor. Even at these parties Waldron never forgot his goal, and when he was feeling his wine he gathered the boys around and told them some of his plans for attacking. Once he even stood in the middle of the room and shouted the single word "attack."

Waldron watched the morale of his pilots like an anxious father. He listed himself in the squadron organization as commanding officer and morale officer. He had molded that group of men by his own determination and singleness of purpose, and he was their leader if anyone ever was a leader. Nobody in the squadron ever called him anything but "Skipper" or "Captain," and no one ever thought of him in any other terms. He had no nickname.

The Skipper looked like an Indian chief, and several members of the squadron told me that part of the blood raging through his veins was of these first Americans. He was middle-aged but still lean and hard.

Jimmie Owens (Lieutenant J. C. Owens, Jr., from Los Angeles, California) was the executive officer. He sat across the aisle from me in the ready room. Brown-haired, with chubby cheeks and a stocky frame, he was the home-loving husband of the group. First of all he loved his wife, and second he was devoted to his work. An Annapolis graduate, he was conscientious in the performance of his squadron duties, which he carried out in a quiet, unobtrusive way. I remember him as soft-spoken and diligent.

Moose Moore (Lieutenant R. A. Moore, from Richmond, Virginia), dark-complexioned, dark-haired Annapolis graduate, sat directly behind me. He was our gunnery officer. He had little to say, but when he did talk he did so in an engagingly shy manner, and there was usually a kind of wistful humor in the content of his words.

Abbie Abercrombie (W. W. Abercrombie, of Kansas City, Missouri) didn't like the idea of flying torpedo planes. He called Torpedo Eight, all too aptly, the "Coffin Squadron" and was always talking about getting out of it, but he never made the effort. Big, sandy-haired, rough-looking Abbie was strictly a "good Joe" and was well liked by all his comrades.

Squire Evans (Ensign W. R. Evans, Jr., of Indianapolis, Indiana) was the smoothie of the squadron. Fresh from Yale, he maintained an aristocratic attitude, but it wasn't affected with him and seemed to suit him quite well. He had a graceful figure and rosy-cheeked, boyish good looks. He still had a crew haircut and wore black and white saddleback Oxfords off duty. His closet was filled with tweed coats and gray slacks.

Waldron was proud to have a "Yale man" in his squadron and often would say, "You boys have plenty of brains and are all well educated. Let's have one of you figure this out and explain it." Then he would call on the Squire to get up in the ready room and talk on some problem in torpedo tactics. Evans, who was our communications and intelligence officer, spoke well and presented his ideas in a lucid manner with logical sequence.

Whitey Moore (Ensign U. M. Moore, of Bluefield, West Virginia) was the squadron clown and Waldron's pet. He had soft, fluffy, blond hair, and his face reminded you of Dagwood's. Everybody liked him immediately—the girls because he was "cute" and they could mother him, the boys because he was witty and unassuming. At squadron parties in Norfolk he used to jitterbug with an intensity that amused the lot. Once when Whitey was asleep in a chair in the ready room, the other boys got some charcoal and painted a mustache on his upper lip. When he woke up he didn't mind particularly, but Waldron came in just then and surprisingly enough got quite angry at the other squadron members for abusing him.

Teats (G. W. Teats, of Sheridan, Oregon), because of his name, had only one logical moniker. But the boys didn't call him this, because Teats was big and strong and insisted that his name be pronounced "Teats." Teats was an individualist who believed in the maxim of live and let live. He was used to running his own life, and he didn't like the Navy to take over for him. He got along all right, though, because he did the work assigned to him and didn't mess in the affairs of others.

Ellison (H. J. Ellison, of Buffalo, New York) looked like a drugstore cowboy or the proverbial collar salesman, because he had slick, dark hair and a thin, girlish face. He was a lot of fun to be with, he talked readily about anything, especially girls, and he was continually laughing. He didn't like to work a great deal, and when the squadron split at Norfolk, half of them to stay behind and train in TBFs under Swede Larsen, who was a driver, and the other half to go to sea under Waldron, Ellison, who had his choice, used to say he was caught between two evils.

The others in that small ready room included Rusty Kenyon (H. R. Kenyon, Jr., of Mount Vernon, New York), a quiet and reserved boy who had married a nurse in Norfolk just before he sailed; G. M. Campbell, of San Diego, California, and J. D. Woodson, of Beverly Hills, California, two lieutenants (jg) who had been promoted from the rank of enlisted chief a short time before; Ensign W. W. Creamer, of Riverside, California, who rarely had much to say except to his personal friends; Ensign J. P. Gray, a tall, well-knit boy from Columbus, Missouri; and one enlisted pilot, R. W. Miles, of San Diego, California.

The above pilots were killed in the forthcoming battle. The only survivor was Ensign G. H. (Tex) Gay. Tex was an ordinary product of Texas, if anyone from Texas is ever ordinary, except that Waldron's training had made a deep impression on him and he was a little more serious than he otherwise might have been. At that time his favorite expression was "horse-meat sandwich," and it had been picked up by all the members of the squadron. What it signified nobody knew.

It was these boys that Waldron was coaching for battle. He posed problem after problem for them to solve. After asking a question the Skipper had a characteristic way of leering out of the corner of his eyes at the squadron, his head cocked, his mouth open in a silly, almost idiotic, fashion. Suddenly he would snap his mouth shut like a trout after a fly, straighten his head, and begin to stroke his chin, staring at them from under his bushy eyebrows and beseeching the answer.

Cruisers, destroyers, and oilers made up our task force. The cruisers are of the *Northampton, Portland,* and *Astoria* classes. Our formation changes all the time. Yesterday we were in a standard cruising formation. The oilers tagged behind. Today we are broken up almost into two forces, with the other carrier group up ahead.

No sight of the Japs yet, although we sighted a sub yesterday. However, this was probably a friendly one. Pilots have orders to identify subs positively before attacking.

Absolute radio silence is in effect, and our pilots on search mission may no longer radio the ship to "spring" them if they get lost and are unable to find the carrier.

Commander Waldron talked to Divine, Karzmar, and me last night. Divine and I will not fly at all, he said, unless there is time to qualify us outside of and beyond regular operations. Karzmar will go on the second torpedo run against the Jap warships if and when we meet them.

Waldron commands the respect of every man in the squadron. He is lean and brown, with the keen eyes and firm mouth of the professional fighting man. He takes care of his men and is continually on the lookout for their welfare. He is well liked for his wry sense of humor. Most important of all, he has a gallant fighting spirit and knows his job thoroughly.

The Skipper has studied the science of torpedo plane warfare to the minutest detail and has indoctrinated all his regular pilots with his knowledge. By means of a "mooring" board he has taught them target leads for any angle of attack and any target speed. All the pilots have worked out so many problems on this board that they carry a mental picture of the track their torpedo will take when they drop. Waldron's "Bible," as he calls it, contains all the information he wants the squadron members to know about torpedo attacks, and apparently every pilot has learned it almost by heart.

Waldron has lost no time in attempting to familiarize the three of us with his methods, and we spend hour upon hour in the ready room trying to catch up on the groundwork the other pilots have acquired during the months of training in the States. If we follow his instructions, the Skipper says, he will guarantee us hits.

Squadron commanders held a conference yesterday afternoon, and last night Commander Waldron called us to the ready room to give us as much information about the situation as he could.

"The approaching battle will be the biggest of the war and may well be the turning point also," he said. "It is to be known as the Battle of Midway. It will be a historical and, I hope, a glorious event."

It is easy to see that the Skipper, who was graduated from Annapolis over twenty years ago, is looking forward to this engagement as the proving point of his career. He is anxious for the torpedo planes to make an especially good showing in order that his painstaking and scientific work on torpedo plane warfare will come to light and be adopted by other squadrons in the fleet, which to date have not gone into the subject as deeply, I believe.

In our ready room we each have a special chair—Waldron's is in the middle in front—and every day we file in and take our seats and begin the day's work, smoking and chatting among ourselves. The Skipper suddenly quiets us down and then in a scholarly and easygoing manner takes up some phase of the torpedo attack. The discussions are leisurely but detailed, and we often spend an hour on some point which seems almost irrelevant. Waldron's method of teaching is very effective. He invites criticism of his theories and allows himself to be talked down, to the point where it seems he must give up and admit he is wrong. Then in a few masterful sentences he proves definitely that his theory is the only one which could be correct. This process keeps the pilots on the alert and rivets in their minds the point he is trying to get across.

Last night Waldron was not sitting in his chair but standing in front of the room. His eyes were twinkling and he grinned as he outlined the plans for our squadron operations. The torpedo planes will make their first attack in the early morning, then return and launch the second attack about eleven in the morning. As many attacks as possible will be made during the day, and then after dark Waldron hopes to make another surprise sally, if he can persuade the command it is feasible. His theory is that the enemy will be in one hell of a mess after the day attacks, with their morale low and confusion rampant. Several ships probably will be on fire to serve as a beacon for our planes. If we can hit them again at night before they can rally it will make them that much more punch-drunk the next day.

This morning the Skipper gave us a few last pointers on fighter evasion tactics, anti-aircraft fire defense, and retirement after the attack. Then he said that he considered the training of his pilots at an end. He told the boys that they had worked with him for so long that he thought of his squadron as "the best in the fleet" and was sure their forthcoming performance would be brilliant. The long hours of training had drawn to a close, and now they were ready to meet the test of combat. From now on, Waldron said, they would give no more drill sessions in the ready room. They were to get as much "sack time" as possible, read, and take it easy like a football team after their last scrimmage and before the big game. We would be called to the ready room again only to keep up to date on changes in the tactical situation.

(Then, as if he knew what was going to happen to the squadron, this hawk-faced fighting man relaxed in his attitude for a moment and urged all the pilots to tidy up their personal affairs and, above all, to write letters to their families, "just in case some of us don't get back.")

Divine and I were told today that we may fly on the third or fourth attack if the captain of the ship will give his permission to let two pilots who never landed a TBD on a carrier take off. I can honestly say I'd like to go to see some action. Furthermore I have in mind the fact that it may be safer to be in the air than aboard this carrier with enemy planes hammering at it. On the other hand, I'd hate to be "cooled" in my first engagement just because I was unprepared in some way. Although I feel I know the plane and its business well enough, I am not used to the tactics of this squadron and might have trouble on that score. I know that as soon as the fighting begins I shall get excited and want to do something. At any rate, the decision of whether I fly or not won't be up to me.

The captain of the "Horny Maru," Captain C. P. Mason, had the following announcement read over the loud-speaker this morning: "The enemy are approaching for an attempt to seize the island of Midway. This attack probably will be accompanied by a feint at western Alaska. We are going to prevent them from taking Midway if possible. Be ready, and keep on the alert. Let's get a few more yellowtails."

Last night all pilots, bombers, and radiomen were called together in the wardroom for an explanation of our strategical situation by one of our senior officers aboard.

Ranged against the Jap forces we have a task force with the *Hornet* and another carrier; another task force with the *Yorktown,* which left Pearl Harbor May 29 to join us at Pt. Luck, 320 miles northwest of Midway; six new Grumman Avenger torpedo planes, which will arrive on Midway today; and three squadrons of Marine fighters on Midway. In addition there are the forces in Hawaii ready to join the battle. Flying Fortresses and other army bombers will be flown to Midway if a need for them develops. Some of them will fly to Midway in any case. Moreover, another of our carriers, which leaves a west coast port today and will make an average speed of twenty knots across, will join the contest if it lasts that long.

Our strategy will be to catch the Japs' main striking force while its planes are flying in toward Midway. Without air protection, the Jap fleet will look like a lot of wet ducks for our fliers. If we knock the carriers out the Jap planes are through as soon as they run out of gas. Then we proceed to demolish the remainder of their fleet—first the striking force, and then the other groups.

Our task force joined the *Yorktown* and her accompanying cruisers and destroyers at Pt. Luck today. Now there are three carriers and many other vessels in our disposition.

Most of the day we spent on the flight deck viewing operations. We watched the other carrier launch her planes. The whole fleet changed course into the wind, and the flagship came slicing past us picking up speed to get wind across the deck. She was about 1,000 yards abeam. The planes taking off seemed to move very slowly across the fore part of the flight deck and float into the air. The aircraft spotted aft looked from a distance like a group of shrub trees with branches springing out a foot or two from the ground. Soon the ship sailed on past us, followed by her guard destroyer knifing through the sea, kicking up snow from her stern. A destroyer is the most graceful of navy craft, I believe. Bucking through the sea with her streamlined bows splitting the waves ahead and a spume of white water rising from the low dip of her freeboard aft, she is what makes sailors want to go back to sea.

On the evening of June 3 most of the members of Torpedo Eight played poker in Ensign Teats's room. They picked up their cards and threw their chips as they always did, some recklessly, some conservatively. They were easy in mind, and when the game broke up they went to bed early and I believe slept soundly.

The battle for Midway started that same night, Wednesday, June 3.

5

The Battle of Midway

TORPEDO SQUADRON EIGHT was in the ready room at about 3:30 A.M. the morning of June 4. Long before the ship was brought to general quarters, pilots and plane crews had been roused for flight quarters and had traipsed into the crowded little room which was their headquarters aboard.

The squadron members had little idea that morning that this was to be their big day. For the most part they slept or drowsed in the comfortable leather chairs, whose back sides let down to reclining angles. Between five and six they began to yawn and wake up and to talk a little. They went down to breakfast in relays, two or three at a time, and thereafter were livelier.

At six-forty the keys on the large teletype screen in the front of the room stirred, and five seconds later a message printed itself out informing the pilots that during the night army bombers and navy PBYs had attacked the enemy main body or support force, consisting of two or three battleships, one carrier, four or five cruisers, and screening destroyers.

The enemy was west of Midway. At that time our three carriers and supporting vessels were northeast of Midway.

This intelligence brought everybody fully awake and held their interest for about an hour. But no elaboration was forthcoming and after a time the pilots relaxed again. They began to tell jokes. I was sitting next to Rusty Kenyon and remember telling him several Limericks, like:

64

There was a young girl from Madras
Who had a beautiful ass,
Not rounded and pink,
As you probably think,
But with long ears, a tail, and eats grass.

The Skipper leaned over to hear them. Then he told one. Kenyon was keeping a collection of Limericks, and he asked us to repeat them and then carefully set them all down on a piece of paper which he put in his pocket.

Whitey Moore, who could sleep at any time, it seemed, was still pounding his ear in the back of the ready room.

Suddenly at eight-ten the battle started for Torpedo Eight. The following message flashed on the teletype screen: "Many enemy planes headed for Midway [from which way] bear 320°."

"This looks like the beginning," the screen told us. "We are about to change course to 330°." From that moment until they climbed into their cockpits the pilots gobbled every sentence off the teletype.

"0815: 8 combat patrol pilots plus two stand-by pilots man planes."

"All fighter pilots man planes on flight deck."

"*Hornet* base course 240°." We had picked up ten knots in as many minutes and were now boiling through the water hell-bent for the Japanese.

Over the loud-speaker came the echoing order, "The enemy main body is now attempting to take Midway. We are heading toward Midway to intercept and destroy them." Already the picture had changed. Now the force was approaching from the northwest instead of from the west. Perhaps the main body had joined the more powerful striking force.

The teletype rattled again, "Pilots of all scout bombers and torpedo planes on flight deck, except squadron commanders, man your planes. Squadron commanders and group commanders remain in ready room for latest instructions. All possible instructions will be sent out by blackboard."

"0825: True surface wind 126° 6 knots. Correction, do not man planes until directed."

"0845: *Hornet* position latitude 31°—368 longitude 176°—29'. Enemy bears 239°."

Orders and vital information streamed onto the teletype screen. Pilots in flight gear were intent over their chart boards working out their navigation.

The loud-speaker blared for all hands to hear. "We intend to launch planes at 0900 to attack enemy while their planes are returning from Midway. We will close to about 100 miles of enemy position."

Again the teletype: "Present intent to launch attack groups 0900 plus 4 sections each carrier for combat patrol. Each group attack one carrier."

Following sound carrier warfare doctrine, some of the fighters were to be sent aloft to protect the ship, others were to accompany the attack groups, and the rest were to remain aboard prepared to relieve the combat patrols or take off to meet emergency situations.

Waldron had been thinking. Now he gave his pilots their last-minute instructions. For some reason, I won't try to guess what, the Skipper had a hunch that the Jap ships would be in a different position than reports placed them, and he told his men that he wouldn't hesitate to run the squadron dry of gas in an effort to find the enemy.

"In that case we'll all sit down in the water together and have a nice little picnic," he said.

"I have no doubt that we'll all be back here by noon," he continued, "but if worst comes to worst and we find ourselves alone and outnumbered by the enemy planes on the way in to attack, we'll keep boring in toward the carrier. If there is only one man left I want that man to take his pickle in and get a hit." Waldron never called a torpedo a torpedo—it was always a pickle, a wienie, a fish, or a torpecker.

After Moose Moore had finished his navigation he began to banter with Ensign Gay, and I overheard him taunt, "You'll never get a hit, Gay. You couldn't hit a bull in the tail with a six-foot rake." Somehow, this was beyond a joke with Gay, and he only answered with a solemn face, "I'll get a hit."

"Man all planes," the final order had come. All pilots hurriedly finished their navigation and clambered one by one out of the ready room. The Skipper was excited. He was about to cap his long years of naval service with a real attack on an important objective. He hunched out of the ready room trying to think of something funny to say but couldn't.

Karzmar was to go on the second attack. Divine and I were to go on the third attack.

But there was no third attack. There wasn't a second attack either. In fact, we never saw any of the planes again after they left the deck.

All the *Hornet* planes were in the air and had left for the target by ten o'clock. Now we had but to wait for their return or for an enemy attack.

It was a beautiful day, the sky a delicate blue with soft clouds on the horizon and the sea sparkling in the sun.

At ten thirty-five the ticker spelled out: "Enemy twin-float seaplane bearing 180. Fighters will investigate. Stand by combat patrol condition one."

All hands had been at general quarters and on the alert long since, but the loud-speaker warned again: "Be prepared to repel an attack."

The threat of one plane was not so alarming, but it might mean a Jap scout had discovered our location and radioed our strength and position back to the Jap carriers. At eleven-twenty, however, word came that the plane had been identified as friendly.

At eleven thirty-five the teletype asserted that the Jap attack on Midway had resulted in little damage to the island and that eight Japanese planes had been shot down.

The first of our planes were sighted returning at one thirty-five. They were SBDs, and when they flopped onto the deck we could see that most of them still carried their bombs. We soon learned that they had not found the Japs and that a few pilots had jettisoned their bombs into the sea.

Our torpedo planes were still out. In another three quarters of an hour they would have to be either on board or in the water, since their gas would be running out by that time. We scanned the horizon for them. Bob Divine and I were on the flight deck.

"Jap planes approaching from astern." Zowie! We forgot

about our torpedo planes. We were about to be attacked, I thought.

"Our fighters are tagging the bandits astern," according to the loud-speaker.

"Stand by to repel attack." Suddenly we saw the attacking planes off the port beam swarming in like a host of bees.

At this point I remember doing a rather foolish thing. I unloosened the flap on my pistol holster, took the .45 out, cocked it, and took a station on the edge of the flight deck prepared to shoot at the Jap planes as they came in. I probably would have been a greater threat to personnel on the *Hornet* than to the Japs.

But the planes weren't after us. They were humming in to sting the *Yorktown*, over the horizon on our port quarter. From afar I saw one smoke smudge and then another where planes had crashed in the water. Two more columns of smoke over the horizon burst up. Then all the planes disappeared. Our fighter planes were being launched.

"Torpedo planes approaching on the starboard bow," came the word. They were Jap planes which had just left the *Yorktown* and were returning. We had not been struck after all but expected to be the next target.

Shortly after this flurry a *Yorktown* fighter made a forced landing aboard. The pilot had been shot in the ankle. He landed in a skid to starboard, his right wheel buckled, and suddenly all six of his .50-caliber machine guns let go in automatic fire.

I was standing on the starboard rail watching the landing and dropped on my back, with three others down in front of me. Karzmar was directly ahead of me. He turned without a word and walked forward to the emergency dressing station. I didn't think he was hurt at the time but believed he had just decided to get the hell out of the place. He had been hit in the mouth and shoulder and peppered with shrapnel. A sailor in front of Karzmar was shot in the knee but not hurt badly. I dragged him to a level place, slit his trouser leg open, and looked at the wound. It seemed only a nick, so I told him to take a look at it. After that he felt better.

There was blood all over me after tending the sailor. I stood up and took a look around. Directly behind me lay the mutilated body of another sailor. He had been hit squarely in the face. The dead sailor lay in great peace, one leg flat on the deck with the toe outturned, the other with his knee drawn up. His arm was outstretched, the palm skyward in a relaxed gesture. "My, he's quiet," I thought. He had returned to simplicity.

I walked on past him to the ladder and saw a Marine sergeant being carried in a stretcher to the dressing room. His right arm was torn badly from shoulder to elbow, and a mess of muscle was exposed. He clutched at his stomach and groaned, "Oooh, oooh" as though it were something he could not comprehend. This was the "shock" I had heard about. The man died that night.

Five men were killed, and more than twenty were wounded by the automatic fire. The startling part of the bloodshed to me was in seeing the naked flesh and skin red and torn. Attendance at the movies made it seem quite normal to see wounded men with blood seeping through their clothing.

Another plane landed soon after this and had automatic fire, this time off the port side, but nobody was hurt.

At two-ten Midway sent word that they were ordering eleven planes from our Bombron Eight (which had landed there after searching for the Japs in the morning) to attack enemy carriers to the northward. We thought perhaps our torpedo planes also had landed on Midway.

Some of our fighters landed aboard, and we heard talk of their battle over the *Yorktown*. The Japs had attacked with torpedo planes guarded by swarms of the dangerous Zero fighters, which are light and maneuverable but go up like tinderboxes when hit, they said.

About four o'clock the Japs attacked the *Yorktown* again, and we were warned: "Stand by to repel attack." Again we watched the Jap planes swarm in over the *Yorktown*. Our fighters took off to join the fray. The *Hornet* had been ignored once more.

At five-ten we were told that the *Hornet* was launching another attack against the Nips (bearing 278°), using our scouts and bombers. The planes, returning after dark, identified the ship by two green glow lights on the west and a string of green lights along the port walkway.

Many *Yorktown* fighter pilots landed aboard during the rest of the afternoon and evening. The *Yorktown* was hit, but not dangerously, although she could take no craft aboard.

At eight o'clock the captain of the *Hornet* passed the word that four Jap carriers were afire and that direct hits had been scored on Jap BBs (battleships) and CAs (heavy cruisers). He gave a "well done" to all hands. He also said army bombers would attack the carriers during the night.

The day's score of Jap losses in their known forces, as later detailed, was: four carriers—all badly damaged; two battleships—one badly damaged, one possibly damaged; four cruisers—one badly damaged; five destroyers—some possibly damaged.

Our forces suffered only heavy plane losses. *Hornet:* fifteen TBDs shot down, three SBDs lost in the water, nine fighters shot down or lost—a total of twenty-seven planes; other carrier: a total of thirty-two planes, including most of their torpedo planes and many SBDs; and *Yorktown:* an undetermined number of aircraft.

Evidently our planes, along with those of other carriers, had won the initial advantage of the battle by putting at least two Jap carriers and one battleship out of commission. Six TBFs from Midway joined in this attack. One returned to the island, the pilot wounded, the gunner dead. The air was lousy with Jap Zeros, he said, and most of our torpedo planes were blasted out of the sky after they had dropped their fish. Apparently our torpecker squadrons struck after the Japs already had returned from Midway and had time to refuel, rearm, and go aloft again.

June 4 was a tough if triumphant day for the pilots on the *Hornet.* Some of them logged more combat hours that day (and the next two) than they ever would again.

After each pilot had landed and made his report he invariably headed for the "admiral's pantry," one deck down from the flight deck, for a drink of lemonade or coffee if neither was available in the ready room. The excitement of combat made everyone thirsty. The returning pilots crowded into their ready rooms or the pantry gulping lemonade out of paper cups, mechanically stuffing sandwiches into their mouths, and at the same time yammering and gesticulating to each other about their individual adventures. Their hair, when they took off their helmets, was matted with perspiration. Their faces were often dirty, and their light cotton flying suits were streaked with sweat. But they were having one hell of a good time. They had fought and won and were still alive, and they felt wonderful. All they wanted to do was go right out and fight again.

They were so excited that their stomachs felt little, and they weren't hungry, but they had to do something so they jammed food into their mouths. Many times that day I saw a pilot, with a cup of lemonade in one hand, two sandwiches in the other, and one side of his mouth packed with bread, try to describe some aerial maneuver, using his hands as opposing planes. It was ridiculous, but for Divine and me it was fun to watch because we couldn't help but catch some of their enthusiasm.

That night after all the attacks were over the pilots gathered in one another's rooms and tried to orient themselves on the day's events.

What had happened to Torpedo Eight? We did not know at the time. We could only be sure that they had sighted and attacked the enemy, because the ship had received Waldron's position report. Upon the basis of this report, flashed back in the morning, the bombing attacks launched during the afternoon had been successfully pressed home. But what of our squadron? How many had come through, and where were they? On Midway? Afloat in rubber boats? Picked up by friendly destroyers or patrol boats? We had no way of knowing.

Bob Divine, ghosting about on the midwatch that same night, saw a small knot of men busied on the hangar deck forward. They were sliding overboard the canvas-cased bodies of the five men killed that day, silently and in the darkness, after a two-minute prayer for each.

June 5 turned up a foggy haze, and we all feared the Japs would either get away or sneak their occupational force into Midway.

Divine and I were up at flight quarters and in our lonely

ready room shortly afterwards. We still didn't know what had become of our squadron, those fifteen pilots and the boys who were their radiomen, but we had begun to know that they were not safe.

At seven-fifteen the commander in chief of the Pacific Fleet sent *Hornet* personnel the word that he was "proud to command you" and added that he estimated "another day of all-out effort on your part will defeat the enemy."

At seven-thirty we received a message over the teletype that we were headed for Midway to intercept Jap forces in case they tried to make a landing.

Later in the morning a radioman from Bombing Eight, who had been on Midway the day before, told us army Flying Fortress pilots gave the torpedo planes credit for hitting two enemy carriers and sinking a battleship, substantiating the claims of the night before.

The radioman said Midway had been badly bombed, contrary to the report of the previous day. The garrison on the island had little water—the supply was distilled from sea water—and little food. Only five planes from three squadrons of Marine fighters were left, and only three were in commission.

One Jap Pilot who was downed on Midway was taped above the abdomen to keep him from blacking out in fast, sudden maneuvers, said the enlisted man. Another story had a Jap fighter in the landing circle at Midway trying to make a pass at an anti-aircraft battery. He was shot down. Jap fighter planes strafed our pilots stranded in rubber boats whenever they found them, according to the Army.

Ten-thirty, over the teletype: "At present we are preparing to attack enemy concentration 50 miles west of Midway."

Eleven forty-five, over the ticker: "It appears the Japs are trying to make a getaway after losses suffered yesterday. All forces are retiring. The occupation force got in to about 150 miles of Midway before turning on its heel and going into reverse early this morning. We are in hot pursuit of some. We hope to put a few transports to the bottom."

The weather began to clear about twelve o'clock. Soon the teletype was in action again. Two o'clock: "We are closing on burning enemy CV [carrier] bearing 320°, distance 240, from Midway in order to polish her off. We are 180 miles from objective. Accompanying CV are 2 BB, 3 to 4 CA."

Two twenty-five: "Estimated that CV is 200 miles distant." All scout bombers were ordered to prepare to launch.

Three o'clock: "Attacked CV first, then damaged BB, then undamaged BB, then CAs. Sinking desired.

"It is believed that originally five Jap CVs were in the Midway attack. Our forces have sighted but four. It is possible that the fifth CV may be in the vicinity of the cripple. Watch out for it."

At four o'clock our scouts and bombers, along with those from the other carrier, took off to intercept the Jap force. The boys were out to "hawk 'em."

We learned nothing of the mission until about eight-thirty, when the first SBDs came in sight on the twilight horizon. They circled the ship and came aboard with the wands. As the light faded and the sky became black the other planes kept streaming in in twos and threes. They came at intervals for an hour or more.

It was cloudy and dark, and the *Hornet* and the other carrier each flashed a searchlight from the tower. The scene was reminiscent of a summer storm on a lake, with the warm, buffeting wind, the darkling clouds, and the lightning stabs of light into the night.

The night landings—for many pilots their first aboard a carrier—were all good save one. Ensign Vammen, from the other carrier, came in without lights on his plane, gunned the motor at the cut instead of chopping it, and hit the barrier. His eye was cut. From him I learned that Jamie Dexter was all right and that Jake the Rake Jaccard had hit the *Akagi* in the middle of the flight deck with a 1,000-pound bomb.

The report from the bomber pilots was not encouraging. They had found and bombed a destroyer, getting two hits out of more than sixty bombs.

At nine that night word was passed over the loud-speaker that one of our VT-8 pilots, Ensign Gay, had been picked up by a U.S. sub. (It was a PBY.) He had said the torpedo attack was a complete success and that he personally made a direct hit on an enemy carrier.

On June 6 we were still tagging the Nips.

The *Hornet* sent out attack after attack against the fleeing Japs. It was a heyday for the dive bombers.

Over the teletype at nine o'clock: "Enemy CV, 500 bearing 239, distance 500 miles from us, spotted. Cruiser planes ordered to search and trail enemy. Prepare to launch attack. We are closing distance."

Ten o'clock: "Scout bombers take off. We may send our cruisers in to the attack if our planes report no air opposition."

Ten forty-five: General quarters.

Eleven forty-five: General quarters.

Eleven forty-five: "Our planes are starting attack."

About twelve forty-five the scouts and bombers returned with the news that there was no carrier but that there were, instead, a damaged BB, a CA, or BB, and six DDs (destroyers). The bombers hit one BB once and the other twice, according to the loud-speaker report. The fighters strafed the destroyers.

Three o'clock: the other carrier, whose group was attacking in intervals while ours was fueling and arming, reported one BB dead in the water, one CA abandoning ship. The *Hornet* planes prepared to polish them off.

Divine and I had by now become very restless at being on board, and we requested the "Sea Hag," the Commander *Hornet* Air Group, Commander Ring, to let us join the dive bombers on at least one attack that day. We had qualified in dive bombing, we told him, and had flown more hours in SBDs than pilots who were returning with accredited hits. He said he would see what he could do, but I could tell by the way he answered that he wasn't going to find time to work us in on some of the fun.

It was fun, too, the pilots said. One flight leader picked up the mike just as he pushed over in his dive.

"Throw everything at 'em but the kitchen stove, boys," he chirped.

A few seconds later the last man to dive came back with: "And here goes the kitchen stove."

Six forty-five: "The following are the results of this afternoon's attack by the *Hornet* group. The BB's magazine exploded as the result of several hits and was on fire from bridge to afterturret. Two more hits were made on the cruiser. A hit was made on one destroyer, and the other destroyer, which remained to rescue survivors, was strafed. The captain can only say, 'Well done, the *Hornet* way.' "

The destroyers were put out of action in a spectacular manner, according to some of the pilots. One was hit squarely in the center with a 1,000-pound bomb and blown completely in two, the forward part diving off at a 45° angle from the after part. Another was turned turtle when a 1,000-pound bomb hit to one side of it. A third was blown out of the sea when a bomb hit her depth charges on the fantail.

On June 7 at flight quarters we learned that the task force had abandoned the chase, if there was anything left to chase, and was headed back toward Midway.

The Battle of Midway was over, but I had no accurate idea of the results, except to know that it was a huge victory for us. The Japanese battle forces which had not been destroyed were in desperate flight for home waters. Our losses in planes had been high, but the annihilating defeat dealt to the enemy had been worth the price many times over. Midway was still ours, and—more important—the Japs would not be able to make another dangerous thrust in the mid-Pacific area for months to come.

We retired eastward after this epic battle, in which the *Hornet* helped sink at least one third the Jap carrier strength and a healthy proportion of her mightiest ships of the line. While the ships in the fleet fueled from the tankers we hung about in a frontal area, with the clouds glowering down to about 300 feet.

On June 9 the captain announced that we were heading north to smoke out the Jap carriers which had been raiding the Aleutians.

The next day the following message was received from Admiral Nimitz, the commander in chief of the Pacific Fleet: "In the Midway battle the performance of *Hornet* and *Yorktown* was superb and consistent with their previous record of brilliant boldness. Their personnel losses I regret far more than those of material. The heroic and grim determination displayed was the decisive factor in producing a great victory for America. The *Hornet* and [other carrier] are now under orders to proceed north and drive the enemy from the Aleutian Islands. I know you will overwhelm the enemy there as you did at Midway, thus insuring his complete defeat."

However, on the following day the *Hornet,* still bound by thick weather, received orders to return to Pearl Harbor and about the middle of June dropped anchor once more in Oahu.

After Midway and on the cruise back the pilots aboard reviewed the events of the struggle and tried to piece together what had happened. We only knew small, isolated details of what had taken place and had no over-all picture of the course of the battle. Bit by bit, as one fits pieces into a jigsaw puzzle, we learned from one individual and another, by rumor and hearsay, what squadrons had attacked what objectives, and the results.

The remainder of Torpedo Eight, those under command of Swede Larsen, flew aboard as we neared Oahu. By that time we knew definitely that Waldron had sacrificed his men and planes in the attack on the Jap carriers (with only Tex Gay surviving) to gain the first advantage of the battle, but we did not know how the attack had been carried out.

The reaction of the pilots to the annihilation of their comrades was one of bewilderment. There was no evidence that they had been killed. The dead just were not there, and it was hard for the others to realize that they never would be.

If there is any one trait that carrier pilots have in common it is matter-of-factness, and I don't think those who remained in Torpedo Eight were as grief-stricken and vengeful as they have been publicized as being. In the Navy, and especially in wartime, you do what you are told to do, and if some of your comrades are killed in the process it's tough to take but it doesn't change you into a wrathful avenger. Eventually, if it happens too many times, it leads to dull despair at thoughts of so many good men dead and to a steadying, cold determination to beat the Japs and win the war. But fancy words don't help. Any time a pilot says, "Thoughts of Jack or Joe will be riding with my next torpedo," he is just blowing or else he is emotionally unfit to be a combat aviator. The only thoughts which should be riding with a torpedo to make a hit are those of entry and departure from the target, target angle, target speed, dropping point, avoidance of A.A. fire, and other matter-of-fact considerations.

On the cruise back to Pearl Harbor, Divine and I had the unpleasant chore of inventorying the effects of the fourteen fliers and fifteen radiomen of Torpedo Eight who had not come back from their attack of June 4. We had to list and pack the clothing and individual articles belonging to each man. Going through every person's private effects—seeing a characteristically battered cap, a girl's picture, an earmarked Prayer Book, or a wallet with various cards in it—in the way that we did made us realize how much each one would be missed at home. It was a disheartening job. We also had to skim through the letters each had received before we sent them back to the nearest of kin, and in them we saw expressed the love and good-luck wishes that seemed so futile now. Many of the officers and men had written last-minute notes, as Waldron advised, and in censoring these—which it was our duty to do, much as we hated prying into them—we found the last heartfelt thoughts of brave men.

As soon as we reached Pearl Harbor all flight personnel were given liberty. Most of the pilots registered at the Moana Hotel or the Royal Hawaiian Hotel, at Waikiki Beach. The Royal Hawaiian has been taken over by the Navy. It is a beautiful place but is restricted to navy men, and no women are allowed in the rooms, there are no dances in the evening, and it doesn't cost enough for anyone who wants to go on a spree. So during the next few days many of the pilots began to spend more time at the Moana, which, since the war, has become a big fun house for the Army and Navy.

The routine of the returning airmen for the next few nights consisted of their tramping from room to room hunting for liquor, talking, arguing, fighting, and breaking the furniture. Some few were feeling tender enough to want to find a girl, but for the most part their emotions were released in being just as mean as they could. I saw two boys who were good friends beating each other in the face with their fists, not trying to duck or box, until they both had black eyes and were crimson with blood. Another pilot tried to throw his smaller friend out of a window. The Moana, which was blacked out, had dim and eerie lights in the hallways, and the scene took on a kind of savage aspect, as though natives were celebrating a ritual.

The navy men felt that they had won the Battle of Midway, but the Army got the play in the Honolulu papers. A running tussle between the two services took place in the Moana, for one place, for a night or two. It was foolish and unpatriotic to argue between ourselves who won. What did it matter, as long as someone did? Dissension and disunity in our armed forces was just what Tojo wanted. So critics said. But the navy pilots were human and they had seen their friends risk and sometimes lose their lives going below 1,000 feet to dive-bomb, torpedo, and sink Jap warships while the Army stayed at a safe 20,000 feet and not only missed but sometimes dropped on our own craft. That's why they got mad at the Army.

I met Dick Jaccard and Jamie Dexter in the lobby of the Moana. Later we got in touch with Bill Pittman and Jerry Richey. They had all been on one of the other carriers.

That night at the Moana Dick's favorite pastime was irritating the house detectives until they chased him through the hallways from floor to floor. He was quick as a gazelle, and when he had easily eluded several of these purple-faced flatfeet he would sneak up behind one of them and goose him, and the chase would start all over again. They finally nabbed him when he tired of this sport and began imitating a superior officer for the benefit of his friends.

At Midway, I discovered, Jake had laid a 1,000-pound bomb squarely on the center of the flight deck of the *Akagi* on June 4 and on each of the following two days had scored a hit on an enemy cruiser. Jamie put a heavy bomb amidships on the Jap heavy cruiser *Mogami*.

Jamie had heard that he and Dick had been recommended for Navy Crosses for their bravery under fire at Midway. (Both were later actually awarded the medals.) "If that's true," said Jamie, "I wish they'd give me two weeks at home instead. I'd make the trade any day. I don't think I'll ever be an ace combat pilot. I suppose I'll make more attacks, but I won't like it."

Jim Shelton did not come back. The last anyone saw of him, he was flying wing in a three-plane section which was retreating after an attack on Jap warships; none of the three planes returned to tell the tale.

I saw Gil Schlendering a few days after we came ashore. He had been on the island of Midway. He was shot down and landed near the island. After floating in his life jacket for two hours he had been picked up and saved. Gil was very quiet the evening I saw him. All the gaiety seemed to have been sapped from him. The little witticisms we tried to cheer him with had no effect and must have seemed superficial to him. Bob Vaupell, who was with him, had not flown from the island. However, many of the boys we had all gone to school with—Ek, Tweedy, Madale, Butler, Sandoval, Swansberger, and others—had been killed.

I saw Tex Gay for just a moment when he came aboard the *Hornet* to get his belongings. I congratulated him on getting back safely but didn't ask him any of the particulars of his experience. The story of the last flight of Torpedo Eight already had been recounted to me by others.

Tex was thin and tired, and his left hand was still bandaged. He gave the impression that he had met and talked to a thousand persons, from admirals to mess boys, since his miraculous return.

I imagine that the last and only attack by Torpedo Eight took place just about as Waldron hoped it wouldn't. When he didn't find the Jap force where contact reports had placed it, he played his hunch, turned westward, and flew until the squadron stumbled on the track of the enemy.

He found the Jap carriers, first sighting them by smoke smudges on the horizon. He made his contact report, thus revealing the exact position of the Jap striking force to our carrier squadron for the first time since early morning.

Then, without hesitating he put his nose down, leveled off just above the water, and went on in. Behind him as he closed toward a volume of Jap A.A. fire were the faithful pilots of his squadron. They knew his caliber, they knew what he was doing. The "worst had come," and they stuck with him. Behind them, after they sighted the Jap fleet, were carrier-based Zeros doing wing overs and half-loops at 250 knots to get into firing position on the tails of the flying freight cars bearing the white star. One by one the TBDs, poking along at 120 knots, crashed into the sea under fire from the Zeros' deadly 20-millimeter cannon. The Skipper went down in flames. Finally there was only one plane left.

"And if this happens I want that pilot to take his pickle in and get a hit."

Tex Gay probably wasn't thinking of Waldron's exact words as he skimmed over the water on that last mile, A.A. raking the sea in front of him, the yellow lines of tracer fire streaking past his wings, and the bulk of one of the biggest Jap carriers looming in front of him. But unconsciously, because of his training under the Skipper and because he was from Texas, this last pilot of Torpedo Eight did just that. Then he flipped his plane over the bow of the carrier and crashed into the water, shot down at last. A few moments later he heard an explosion. It was his torpedo going home.

Gay stayed afloat in his Mae West life jacket till sundown and then inflated his rubber boat and clambered in. What he saw that day was the successful follow-up of Waldron's suicidal attack. Tex watched as American dive bombers, tipped off to the Japs' position by Waldron's radioed report, went down on the Jap carriers while the enemy planes refueled and rearmed.

A PBY picked Gay up the next day.

Commander Waldron has been criticized for recklessly sacrificing an entire aircraft squadron, both men and material, but especially men, in a suicidal attack which had no hope of success and could only be a gesture.

His critics, I believe, do not fully understand the tactical situation prevailing that day. The Jap striking force of three carriers and supporting warships had not been sighted for four hours when Waldron caught up with it. A fleet can move over one hundred miles in any direction in that time. It was important that our carrier aircraft find this force before it softened Midway to the point at which the island could be occupied and before their aircraft discovered our carriers.

Waldron's main contribution to the course of the battle was in locating the enemy fleet, not in his do-or-die attack, glorious as that was. Perhaps the reason Waldron thought the

Japs would be westward of their reported position lay in the fact that they had been discovered and hit the night before and that morning. What more natural than that they should retire until the fires were under control and they had redesigned their plan of attack? This is just a guess.

At any rate, Waldron was right. He, of all the squadron commanders and of the higher-ranking officers who direct the squadron commanders, figured out where the Jap fleet was and confirmed his reasoning by finding it.

I am sure he made his decision on the combat reports which flowed in during the early morning. In the cagey brain of this trained fighting man evolved the correct answer to the question which was bothering everyone that morning, namely, "Where is the Jap fleet?"

Why, then, once he had sighted the fleet and radioed in his report as to its location, didn't he wait until the support of dive bombers and fighters would allow him to make a combined attack with a reasonable chance of scoring several hits and making a getaway?

In the first place, according to the tactics then practiced, the fighters were at altitude with the dive bombers and none were with the torpedo planes. The two groups, fighter-bomber and torpedo planes, became separated on the flight out, since they were at different levels. To wait for the fighter-bomber group was useless as far as fighter protection for the torpedo planes was concerned, since the fighters would stick with the bombers. On a co-ordinated attack some of them were supposed to come down with the bombers and then escort the torpedo planes in to drop. Waldron suspected that these tactics would not afford much cover for the torpedo planes, and he always told his boys he "hoped" they would have a fighter escort, but he built his attack on the theory that the torpedo squadron would be alone.

To wait to strike with the dive bombers would disperse the enemy's A.A. fire and thus give the torpedo planes much more of a chance to get in, drop, and get out. Waldron knew this. He was an expert on torpedo plane warfare, and it must have been obvious to him that an unsupported rush by his squadron against a large surface force, while it might net some hits, almost certainly would result in the destruction of most of the planes.

Waldron's philosophy of "attack and attack again" undoubtedly had a great deal to do with his decision. But there might well have been other considerations. If he went in close enough to make a complete estimate of the size, the make-up, and the disposition of the enemy fleet it was more than likely enemy fighters would discover and jump him anyway. It was vital to our command to have this information. Waldron gave it to them and then proceeded to the attack instead of turning tail and running the grave risk of having the squadron shot up on the way out instead of on the way in. Finally, he probably was low on gas and couldn't afford to wait longer for the dive bombers and maintain any hope of getting back to the carrier afterwards.

Sixteen other members of Torpedo Squadron Eight had died at Midway on June 4 in an attack on the Jap carrier group made four hours before Waldron's fifteen planes headed in on their last run. Six TBFs, each carrying a pilot, a turret gunner, and a radioman-bombardier, left Midway shortly after dawn and hit the Jap carrier force at seven o'clock in the morning. They were from the other half of Torpedo Eight—that commanded by Lieutenant H. H. Larsen—which had remained in Norfolk to train in the new torpedo planes when Waldron's outfit put to sea. One of these six planes returned to Midway and crashlanded on the field. The other five were shot down. The pilot of the surviving craft, Ensign A. K. Earnest, told me the story of this first of two reckless efforts by Torpedo Eight to stop the Jap fleet.

Bert Earnest is tall and lean, with black hair, dark eyes, and tanned skin. Many people think he is handsome because of this combination. He is from Richmond, Virginia, pronounces "out" as "aout," and believes in being gallant with the ladies.

He is literal-minded, and it is this quality that makes him an exceptionally fine aviator. Bert likes to know from a mechanical and practical standpoint just what will or what has taken place, and he's not interested in romanticizing facts to make a good story. Because he thinks quickly, "A. K." is one of the best in the cockpit. He has risked his neck many times since Midway, but even though he is prepared to do so again, he says quite frankly that he won't enjoy it.

Bert and five other pilots of Larsen's detachment flew from Pearl Harbor to Midway three days before the battle. They were glad they were chosen to go, because it gave them some respite from Larsen's continual needling. They all liked to serve under "Feeb" (Lieutenant L. K. Fieberling), the dashing, even-humored executive officer of the squadron. In the States Feeb used to wow the girls. He drove a sleek Lincoln Zephyr convertible, his "passion wagon," and was always well groomed and mannerly. The flecks of gray in his dark hair belied his youth and gave him a distinguished appearance. The boys liked him because he was not temperamental and was always straightforward in his dealings with them. It was Feeb who christened Larsen "The Lion."

The other four were happy-go-lucky Charlie Brannon (Ensign C. E. Brannon), a lanky and humorous lad with an open heart who had married only two weeks before he left Norfolk; Vic Lewis (Ensign V. A. Lewis), the schoolteacher from Boston who enjoyed constructing complex sentences with big words for the benefit of his squadron mates; Oz Gaynier (Ensign O. J. Gaynier), who always appeared to be worried about something and whose wife, Rita, still thinks he is a Jap prisoner and will turn up after the war; and an enlisted pilot, short, stocky Woodside.

At four-thirty in the morning of June 4 these boys and their radiomen and gunners had manned their planes and warmed them up. Then they cut their engines and began to nod in the cockpits as the fading darkness slowly unveiled the sandspit on which the field lay. They had not had their breakfast yet, and they were waiting for the warm glow which the first swallow of hot coffee would bring.

At about five-thirty a Marine officer wakened Bert, who was fast asleep under his hood, and told him to stand by for take-off. A navy patrol plane had reported the presence of enemy aircraft in the vicinity. Even then Bert didn't think they were going out.

But Feeb had started his engine, so Bert turned his motor up too. The fighters were taking off as Feeb began to taxi out. The TBFs followed the fighters into the orange sky, and behind them four army B-26s roared down the runway.

The TBFs set course 320°, Feeb in the lead, with Earnest and Brannon on his wings, and Oz Gaynier leading the second section with Vic Lewis and Woodside.

The planes were not ten minutes out on their heading when two enemy craft plummeted out of the brightening sky above them and made a pass. Earnest thought they were Messerschmitt fighters (Me. 109s). They made only one run, firing all the way in, but didn't hit anybody.

Earnest and Brannon thought this was fun. Across the tail of Feeb's plane they exchanged their own version of the squadron's attack signal (arm extended with closed fist) by raising an arm and closing the fist except for the second finger, the goosing finger.

Then A. K. looked back toward Midway and saw A. A. fire and a plane burning in mid-air. It looked like the McCoy, he thought.

The six torpedo planes kept humming toward their objective, unescorted and vulnerable, just as the other section of Torpedo Eight was to do four hours later. They were flying just below the clouds at about 4,000 feet when Bert caught sight of the Japs. What he saw at first he took to be a transport. Nice pickings. Then gradually the extent of the Jap fleet became apparent, as the carriers and the disposition of light cruisers and destroyers ringing them came into focus out of the morning haze.

"Here they come," Manning (Earnest's radioman) shouted over the interphone, and suddenly from twenty-five to thirty Zeros poured out of the clouds on top of them, from all sides. Manning fired fifty rounds, and then they got him with a 20-millimeter shell right through the chest.

Bert opened his bomb bay doors. There were Zeros all over them now. They came in from the front too, often passing over the torpedo planes on their backs and then rolling out in a half-loop to jump the tails of the Americans. Bert saw tracers, he saw big red balls of fire bursting out on his wings, and he saw nasty sparks streaking through the sky. The place was alive with lead.

He leaned out of the cockpit to look back, and a bullet

pinked his jawbone. He could hear the pitter-putter-putter of bullets against the armor plate behind his head.

Ferrier, his radioman, called to say he had been hit in the head, a skull wound that dazed him.

A shell punctured the hydraulic system, and the tail wheel of the plane fell down, blocking out the tunnel gun and making it useless. Cannon holes were making cheese graters out of the wings.

"Then my flags started flying," said Bert. The red metal flags, indicating that his wings, which are of the folding type on the TBF, were unlocked, popped up.

Bert and the others kept nosing in with the Zeros, mincing at them on the way. About five miles inside the outer screen of ships a shell tore away Bert's elevator control cable, the stick fell limp in his hand, and the plane began to glide toward the water.

"I veered out of the formation," Bert said, "and tried to control my altitude with my rudder and ailerons, but it didn't work. I thought I was all through, so I aimed my torpedo as best I could at the nearest ship, a four-stacker light cruiser of the *Jintsu* class, and dropped. Then, just as I was about to hit the water I rolled back on my elevator tab and the plane leapt toward the sky again."

An elevator tab is an elevator on the elevator, and it fixed the altitude of the plane just as the elevators themselves do. It is used to trim the craft in flight. Bert's remembering to try it saved his neck that day.

Two of the Zero pack had singled out Bert's plane when he left the formation, and as he fled through the A.A. fire from the screening vessels they tagged after him. They chased him for more than twenty miles.

"I tried everything I had ever heard of to avoid their fire," Bert explained. "I sideslipped, I chopped the throttle, I turned and twisted and jinked. Finally they ran out of ammunition and left me."

Earnest never did see what happened to the other planes. I heard a rumor later, however true, that an army Flying Fortress was shadowing the fleet at the time and saw one of the planes crash into a carrier and spotted a cruiser smoking.

When he was in the clear Bert began to figure out how to

get back. His electric compass had been shot up and was useless. The Jap fleet was between him and Midway.

"I don't know whether we'll ever get back," he told Ferrier, "but we're sure as hell going to try."

Using the sun, which was still low on the eastern horizon, as a directional guide, Bert by-passed the enemy ships, headed straight south till he thought he was opposite Midway, and then turned eastward.

The cloud shadows on the water played him tricks, and many times when he thought he had seen the island it turned out to be but the outline of another cloud on the sea. Just when he was sure he was becoming hopelessly lost he saw a big black cloud of smoke on the horizon. It was from the fires on Midway. He headed toward it and lost altitude. Suddenly he spotted the tiny island of Kure, seventy miles west of Midway, and he knew where he was.

When Earnest came in to land at Midway they waved him off with a "wheels not down" signal, but Bert knew he had dumped his wheels so he came around again. This time an officer on the field was smart enough to invent a signal for "one wheel not down." He put one arm straight up and folded the other across his chest.

Bert thought he understood, but on the next pass he watched the spectators as he came in. He reasoned that they wouldn't know whether he had dropped his torpedo or not and would start running to escape a possible explosion if both his wheels were up.

So Bert headed his shell of a plane up the groove. With his stick flapping around in the cockpit, his flaps still up, a dead gunner and a wounded radioman riding with him, he controlled the landing by the clumsy tabs, until he was in position to hit the field. The spectators were not running. Only one wheel was not down. The airplane eased on to the runway, the asphalt tore at the underbelly, the prop bent to a curlicue, and then the plane swerved to the right and came to a halt. The fight was over for Bert Earnest and for five of his comrades in Torpedo Eight.

There were bright spots, though. Tommy Durkin was back in Pearl Harbor, recuperating after having spent fourteen days in a rubber boat. The way he told the story it was funny, but I'm sure it must not have been. He was lost, he said, northeast of the New Hebrides. After setting the plane down he and his radioman pulled themselves into the rubber boat and soon were alone in the desert of ocean. They had water and two days' emergency rations.

The first five days were not bad, Tom said, but after that time dragged and hope waned.

"I had won a lot of money—about $220—playing poker the night before we were lost," Tom told us, "and when we began to get really thirsty after the fifth day I amused myself by counting it over in front of the radioman, estimating how many milkshakes it would buy at fifteen cents a shake. Then I remembered a place in the States where I could buy milk shakes at five cents a glass, so I went through the calculations all over again. After that I thought maybe I'd prefer lemonade or orangeade and was about to figure out how many gallons of that I could buy, when I looked at my radioman. He was fingering his knife, and he had a queer look in his eye. I stopped, because I was afraid he wanted to eat me."

Tom lost hope on the tenth day. The two drank the rest of their water and waited. On the eleventh day they saw land, Espiritu Santo, the northernmost large island in the New Hebrides group. Three days later they reached shore. Tom's radioman caught an eel in a pool and, holding it by either end, took a bite right out of the middle while it was still wriggling. For three days more they lived on shellfish as they staggered their way down the beach. At last they found a native hut, entered, drank some coconut milk, and then fell sound asleep on the grass matting inside. The natives found them there and returned them to the nearest navy base.

Tom is a Catholic. He said he made so many vows as he was saying his rosary during those fourteen days that he was going to have a tough time living up to them the rest of his life.

6

Off on Another Mission

A SHORT TIME after the *Hornet* returned to Pearl Harbor I was transferred back to Torpedo Squadron Three, which I had come to think of as my old squadron. Torpedo Three had been sent out to Midway on the *Yorktown* and had suffered losses in planes and personnel almost as heavy as those of Torpedo Eight. Only two pilots, Corl and Esders, returned from the attack. The others were shot down.

Bill Esders, who was flying wing on Lieutenant Commander Massey, his skipper, said the latter stood up in his cockpit trying to get out after a direct hit in the engine threw a sheet of flame back over the fuselage. Bill himself was chased by Zeros for many miles and shot full of holes. He landed in the water near the listing *Yorktown* and was picked up. His radioman died in the rubber boat. Bill told us that while he was huddled in this tiny craft a Jap plane sighted him and came in to strafe but abandoned his sport when a Grumman dropped down on his tail.

Torpedo Three, with Lieutenant Commander J. M. Jett as skipper, and a nucleus of the pilots who had not flown at Midway—Lieutenant Johnny Myers, Lieutenant Konig, "Weasel" Weissenborn, Jerry Stablein, Fred Herriman, Hank Schneider, John Armitage, and the enlisted pilots, Baker, Corl, Weis, and Esders—began training again at Kaneohe. This time we had a new plane to fly. It was the Grumman Avenger, the TBF, a bigger, faster, better-armed torpedo plane than the TBD. It looked so big to us that at first we

88

called it the "Monster." It was a beautiful plane to fly, however. Everything worked hydraulically if not electrically, and, once mastered, the cockpit was as simple as a one-way street. In this torpedo plane we could outclimb, outdive, and turn inside our own Grumman fighters, which were, however, more maneuverable. We could find only one or two faults with it. There were not enough guns forward. The stick controls were stiff. But otherwise this big, clumsy-looking craft was a dream and amazed us every day with what it would do.

While we were in training at Kaneohe, Hank Schneider took off in an SBD one day and flew over to Ford Island. On the way back, just off Diamond Head, he got tangled up in a friendly dogfight with some army P-40s. Finding himself on his back below 1,000 feet, he tried to pull the plane through in a half-loop instead of rolling out. He hit the water in a dive in full view of the bathers on Waikiki Beach and was killed.

Part of our training in the new planes consisted of qualifying aboard a carrier. The squadron flew out to sea south of Oahu one day, and each pilot made three landings apiece. The TBF turned out to be a wonderful carrier plane. It landed like a leaf and often was in the air on take-off by the time it passed the first elevator.

We had only one accident that day. Lieutenant Konig landed slowly a little too far to the starboard side of the deck, and the wash of the wind from the stacks caught one wing and threw him on his back over the side and into the sea. All three occupants escaped from the plane and were picked up by a destroyer. Konig said that he came to the surface under the wing and thought for a moment, "Holy Christ, I'm under the ship!"

Torpedo Three went to sea aboard the same carrier on July 15. The "Big E," the carrier *Enterprise,* was part of a task force consisting of a large new battleship and accompanying cruisers and destroyers. I was glad to be on this particular carrier, because there were many officers in other squadrons aboard whom I knew well. Jamie Dexter, Dick Jaccard, Bill Pittman, Hoot Gibson, Micheel, Richey, and Kline were among those I knew in the bombing squadron, and Harry March and Willie Wileman were in the fighter squadron.

The ship was heading south to waters I had never seen before. Tongatabu, in the Tonga Islands, southwest of Samoa, was our immediate destination. But after that we were off on another mission toward we knew not what nor where. The ship's crew and deck personnel were apparently efficient and experienced, and the ship itself already had a fighting reputation. Altogether, I was very pleased to be aboard.

At sea again I fell into the simple routine of eating, sleeping, reading, sun-bathing, and, of course, flying. Flying on a cruise is for the purpose of guarding the task force, by 150- to 250-mile-searches relative to the ship, in case of torpedo planes. On the return from searches offensive exercises were carried out by all squadrons. The torpedo planes conducted simulated torpedo attacks on the carrier, practiced dropping small sandbags containing messages on the flight deck, and fired at a sled towed by the carrier or a sleeve towed by another plane. The scouts and bombers practiced dive-bombing and the fighters strafing. All squadrons were taking advantage of the time available on the cruise southward to perfect the individual skill of the pilots and the co-ordination technique of units.

In the TBF there are two crew members besides the pilot, namely, the turret gunner, who squeezes himself into the small gun turret, the "goldfish bowl," sitting above the tail, and the radioman-bombardier, who sits in the bombardier's compartment in the belly of the ship behind the torpedo or bomb load. Usually the same crew flies together all the time, so that they get to know each oher, and can co-operate more efficiently.

I was lucky in being assigned two good men. Ferrier, who had been Earnest's radioman at Midway, had been transferred to Torpedo Three and was my turret gunner. He still wore the marks of that battle. On his scalp just above his forehead on the right side a circular expanse of skin gleamed through his close-cropped hair like a shiny half-dollar. That was where a bullet had flirted with his brain. He was obviously impressed by his experience at Midway. I felt that he was more subdued than he normally would have been, as though the death he had seen sprayed through the air that day had knocked the wind out of him for a while.

"I have no hankering to be an ace gunner and shoot down fifty Japs," he told me. "All I want to do is put enough .50-caliber slugs in the air to keep the Zeros off our tail." This made it evident that he didn't regard the war as a pulp fiction adventure but as a matter of doing his job and getting back. He had learned in combat that Jap planes will turn away when their pilots see .50-caliber tracers looping too close.

In the air Ferrier didn't talk much over the interphone; he merely sat hunched up in the turret with his knees under his chin, smoking cigarettes and being quietly glad he was alive.

Deitsch, who was my radioman, hadn't had combat experience, but he was a thorough and conscientious worker. He always kept our plane shipshape and clean, and when he wasn't otherwise busied I would see him on the hangar deck wiping it down with a rag. His job only entailed tending and operating the radio and bombing gear, so that this activity demonstrated his real pride in the plane itself. He looked chubby because of his chipmunk cheeks, but his body was rugged rather than fat. This and his stubborn, steady will helped him put up a brave and inspiring fight for life when he was wounded later.

Deitsch liked to make up his own mind and do things his own way, which was generally very competent, and it worked out much better if I told him to do something and let him do it for himself than if I tried to explain how to do it. But there were some things we had to talk over in order to co-operate efficiently, and for this reason Deitsch and Ferrier often used to come up to my room in the evenings. Normally they stayed in their quarters below decks with the other enlisted men.

In these sessions we went over the duties of each man in the plane during every phase of a torpedo attack. For example, Deitsch was to man his tunnel gun on the initial approach, check his switches and remind me to open my bomb bay doors as we headed down, and call "Torpedo away" when the fish dropped. Ferrier, in the turret, was to keep me informed of what was going on behind us, and I was to let them both know all I could of the developement of the attack.

We tried to imagine what we would do in every conceivable situation—if we were forced to make a water landing, if we were shot down, if we had to bail out, if one of us was wounded, if our plane was attacked by two or thirty Zeros, etc. In this way we all knew pretty much what to do and didn't have to waste valuable time deciding in the air—we practiced this co-operation as much as possible on the long searches we made every day.

A single plane search to any distance is an unusual experience, and there is cause for some excitement on every flight. Once settled down on the first leg of a search, the pilot can stop watching his compass heading and air-speed so closely and look about him. His main purpose in searching is to see what's there and report it back to his ship.

Perhaps he will be cruising at about 1,000 feet, just below puffball convection clouds, white or tinged yellow and pink by the rising sun. It is hot, and he has his shirt neck open and his sleeves rolled up and maybe, if he doesn't mind the noise, his cockpit enclosure pushed back, with the breeze rushing past and the motor thrumming in his ears. He can look in every direction without seeing more than trackless water spotted by a haphazard pattern of cloud shadows. It often seems to him that these shadows can be used to establish direction, but he realizes that this is only an illusion natural to land-bred fliers. Through the good, acrid stench of gas and oil that he has come to love cuts the smell of cigarette smoke, and he knows his gunner is puffing on the cheap brand of tobacco he uses.

At the end of the first or second leg the pilot sometimes drops a smoke bomb to determine wind direction or to set a target for free and fixed machine gun fire. Cannonading at this target out in a void of water and sky where only he and his crew hear the noise gives him an eerie feeling, a little as though he were yelling in the woods.

The third, or intercept, leg is the crucial leg because it either does or does not bring the plane back to the carrier. Just as the pilot searches the water on the first leg, scanning the horizon for any sign of ship or plane and watching the ripples in the sea to fix his wind direction, so he does on the third leg to find his carrier. If he has done his navigation correctly and "Pt. Option" has not changed without his knowing it, the fleet will appear at the proper time. If not, there is still only water and more water.

The fleet reveals itself to the pilot in different ways. Sometimes the carrier stack will stand out as the tiniest of regular smudges on the horizon. Sometimes the wake of a large vessel or the combination of several wakes forming straight white lines strikes the eye. A flash of sunlight reflection may give the force away, or the ships may suddenly emerge as small gray slivers on the water. Whenever there is a straight line or regular form on the water it can be taken as something more than the sea itself. Usually the pilot can see the fleet from five to twenty minutes before he reaches it.

Four days after we left Pearl, Jamie Dexter was lost. He took off about twenty minutes to three in the afternoon, not thirty miles from the equator, to tow a sleeve for our fighters to make runs on. He was towing about ten miles to starboard of the fleet. When the fighters left him he presumably dropped the sleeve and climbed to about 8,000 feet above the clouds to join the rest of his squadron in a strafing attack on a sled towed by the carrier. Then he must have lost sight of the fleet.

I was in the wardroom eating dinner when I heard that Jamie was missing. I threw my napkin on the table and hurried topside to air plot, the aircraft nerve center of the carrier, in order to find out as much as I could about the circumstances of his flight. From their plot of his aircraft after he became lost the officers in air plot surmised that Jamie at first had flown a square in order to locate the fleet, then abandoned this method and taken up a course away from the carrier (apparently he thought the ship was on the opposite side of him to what it actually was), and finally struck out for the nearest land, the Phoenix Islands. When last detected, he was some distance from Enderbury, the nearest of these islands.

The ship's commander did everything possible to rescue Jamie without endangering the fleet security. The carrier broke radio silence several times—even more often than was prudent—to give him his course to steer back to the ship. Three times I heard them call by voice: "Dexter, in [such and such plane], steer [such and such course]." They even changed the entire fleet course at about seven o'clock and headed toward him for a time in order to close the gap between plane and carrier.

Jamie and I had had lunch together that day and afterwards took a sun bath on the walkway on the portside of the flight deck. We began talking about being lost, and we wondered whether the ship would come back for a plane if it was lost. We decided that on this cruise, at least, it wouldn't. Jamie said that once he knew he was lost with no chance of finding the carrier he would head for the nearest land, and I imagine that is exactly what he did.

The more experienced carrier officers seemed to think Jamie made two mistakes. In the first place, he flew generally in a direction 180° away from the fleet when he should have known and remembered which side of the fleet he was on. In the second place, he violated an old pilot's rule of thumb to fly upwind when lost.

But there is no telling what was in Jamie's mind as he made his course changes. It is easy to sit on the carrier in front of a chart and say what the pilot should do, but it is more difficult to think as clearly and easily with nothing but empty sky and sea and cloud shadows for a guide.

One thing Jamie did not do that many pilots might have done with their neck at stake: because those were his orders, Jamie did not break radio silence. No transmission ever was heard from his plane, although five receivers on board were tuned to his frequency.

We all had great hopes that Jamie would be found. We knew he had a good head and imagined that if he were able to make a safe water landing and get into his rubber boat we might find him or he would drift with the favorable trade winds into the islands.

But although next day we made a thorough honeycomb search in the area, no trace of him was ever found. And later, when we began soberly to estimate his chances of drifting over two hundred miles into one of eight islands fifty or more miles apart, none of which are more than ten miles long or twenty-five feet above sea level, the prospect of his survival seemed miserable. What is more likely, he wasted away, he and his radioman, alone under an equatorial sun on an endless ocean, broiling by day and chilled by night, parched and swollen with thirst and crowded by despair until madness or death was merciful.

Jamie's loss took the fun out of the cruise for quite a while.

We had crossed several weather zones on the trip southward, and the changes in wind and climate were stimulating to the imagination. Honolulu, in 20° N. latitude, is in the band of the northeast trades, and there the breeze blows cool and strong all day. At 10° N. latitude we reached the southern limit of the northeast trades and entered the area of the intertrade fronts, where the wind is variable and it is hotter. Then we reached the doldrums, where to our surprise there were no dead calms, although we did notice a definite slackening of the wind. The heat was not overly oppressive. We picked up the southeast trades at about 02° north of the equator. The heat of the equator was not what I expected but the sun seemed very large and near.

When we crossed the equator Neptunus Rex was not invited aboard to supervise the initiation of the "polliwogs" (those who have never crossed the line) by the "shellbacks" (those who have been over before), because of the war.

Living on a carrier became very satisfactory to us after a week or two out. There were eating and sleeping and smoking and the weather to think about. There was time to enjoy the smaller luxuries—a cigar, eliminating, a hot shower, or spitting downwind—and everybody had more time for himself and others. We didn't have to look at the dishware ads or go from one place to another or get drunk. All the evils of the shore—and, as McFee said in his *Casuals of the Sea,* "all the real evils of the world are bred ashore"—were left behind. Women—all of them—for most of the men aboard tended to merge into a rosy composite of Hedy Lamarr and the Virgin Mary, and in this abstraction they seemed their most delightful.

There were health and high spirits out there, but the cares of money and the feverishness of business were no longer.

The days slid by. Life was natural. And there were always the clean strong wind and the restless sea.

Fresh water was precious, because every drop had to be distilled from sea water and the apparatus could make only so much every day. We continually received warnings to conserve water by not standing under the shower nor letting the basin tap run. All water was turned off during general quarters. Every day the water consumption per man per day was published, and this, curiously enough, was one of the things we became interested in. The average was about eighteen gallons.

At night, since there were no flights, we had the time to ourselves and usually gathered in one another's rooms to toss the ball around or to play cards. I often went into Jaccard's room, which was next door, and ordinarily found Gibson and Pittman and Micheel there too. Jaccard had roomed with Tommy Durkin until he was lost and thereafter with Jamie until he too failed to return, and Dick joked about this as though he were a jinx for his friends.

We talked about where we were going (nobody knew at the time), about amusing things that had happened to us in the past and what we were going to do when we got back and after the war, and about girls. Pittman never had any doubt about his future. The first move he intended to make was to marry "Little Natalie," and after that everything would take care of itself. Jaccard had been to architectural school and evidently been quite a promising draftsman and designer, and he had some vague idea of continuing in that line. The evidence we had of his ability was in his habit of sitting idly and drawing cartoons as we talked. Hoot Gibson and Micheel didn't have any definite programs. "After the war" was too far away to think about.

Sometimes we played poker or red dog, a put-and-take game which sounds innocent in explanation but costs tens and even hundreds of dollars to a heavy loser. Generally, everybody retired before ten or eleven o'clock in order to be up for flight quarters before dawn the next day.

In the daytime when we weren't flying or engaged in other squadron duties it was fun to lie in the signal officers' net forward, watching the bow rise and fall and the flying fish skitter across the water ahead of the ship while the sun beat down on our backs. Many of the pilots were veteran "sack artists" and hit the pads during the day to read or sleep whenever they knocked off work. Once in a while some of the boys put on the gloves and boxed in the passageways, but most just relaxed whenever they got the opportunity.

On July 23 as the carrier was approaching Tongatabu two TBFs and one F4F took off and flew 168 miles to the island.

Tongatabu, measuring about twenty-five by ten miles, is the largest of about 180 islands in the Tonga (meaning friendly) group, which lies between the Samoan and Fiji groups, south of both.

We were flying in to the island to give two of our newer pilots field carrier landing practice. Corl was piloting one plane, with Signal Officer Dobson, Ensign Holley, and a radioman as passengers, and I flew the other, carrying Lieutenant Commander Burrough, chief of Admiral Kincaid's staff, who had some official business ashore, and Ensign Schild. Nobody ever figured out why the fighter came along.

The field at Tongatabu is of grass over clay, and it is quite large. A squadron of P-40s was based there. The panorama reminded me immediately of pictures I had seen of AVC fields in Burma. The vegetation around the field was largely coconut palms, tall grass, and many-limbed shade trees. Planes were set in crude revetments around the field and camouflaged with nets covered with leaves. The operations building was a bamboo shack with grass thatching. The tower was a small bamboo hut set on the stumps of coconut palms. The propeller shop, parachute loft, assembly and repair shops were out in the open under the trees.

The Army's quarters were back in the jungle, some quarter-mile from the field. That evening—a lovely tropical night with the moon pale above and the fragrant smell of the woods perfuming the cool air below—we sat about in tents and shot the breeze with the army pilots. They produced some Australian beer, which they said was 20 per cent alcohol. It was exceptionally good, and after one or two quarts our tongues were liquid.

The army fliers told us about the native queen, Salote Tabu (the name sounds like an advertisement for salad dressing), an enormous woman of 290 pounds, who ruled over the kingdom of Tonga with a firm hand. She was a member of the international W.C.T.U. and frowned on all stimulated gaiety. They said she lived in a cave now, although she had a beautiful home on the island.

The army boys complained of having nothing to do in the way of recreation. The swimming was poor because of coral. It was a court-martial offense to toy with the native women, unattractive as they were. Besides, Salote Tabu had driven the young girls back into the hills just to make sure no American would risk martial punishment.

The next day we drove in an army command car to Nukualofa, on the other side of the island. Nukualofa, the largest settlement and capital of all the Tongas, rims the harbor of the island. On the way over we got a glimpse of the natives and their homes. The natives were stocky and burly, with thickish ankles and wrists and negroid faces. They were Melanesian rather than Polynesian. They all wore skirts (including the men), which were made of bright-colored calico cloth or of the matting of palm leaves. Very small children, however, wore nothing at all and ran wild in front of their homes with the pigs and dogs of the family. The skin of these people is a dark, rich brown.

Almost all the Tongans live in oval-shaped huts of coconut palm leaf matting or bamboo topped with grass thatching. Schools and churches, all rectangular and painted white, constituted the only other type of building on the island. The two are incongruous.

The island must have been truly a tropical paradise before the whites came. It is a coral formation, about sixty feet high, covered with palms, cooled by the trade winds, fostering an abundance of food, and peopled by friendly natives. Two or more lagoons in the center and the coral-lined bay, shallow for the most part, radiate brilliant blues and greens.

Now the natives, I understand, are suffering from tuberculosis and other diseases. I noticed that their faces were uglier because their eyes looked tired. In Nukualofa itself many now wore slovenly cheap dresses instead of their regular attire. In this small harbor town they shuffled around in bare feet, selling fruit and post cards for "a dollah," the only unit of American currency they seemed to know.

A spot named "Tonga Lil's," which sounded as though it might produce some trouble, turned out to be a drab coffee shop managed by a watery-eyed, tired old native woman.

They appear unwholesome and dirty in town but less so in the bush, where they lead lives more normal to them. Even so, I saw only one attractive-looking native while I was there. She was a slim, clear-faced creature of about twelve whose bare breasts were just budding. We passed her in the command car, and I gulped but had to go on talking to a superior officer about the flora and fauna of the island.

There is an abundance of fruit and vegetables on the island, including coconuts, bananas, pineapples, avocados, peanuts, papaya, mangoes, yams, peas and beans. The natives eat a lot of pork, and pigs are evident everywhere. The only novelty of animal life on the island is a fruit-eating bat, which I never saw.

On Saturday, July 24, we flew back aboard the carrier, hitting the deck just as she was leaving the harbor mouth. The next day we had crossed the international dateline and it was Sunday, July 26.

7

Approaching the Solomons

THE DAY AFTER our task force sailed out of Nukualofa it effected a rendezvous with two other task forces, each composed of a carrier and supporting war vessels. A large number of transports carrying Marine shock troops also joined us. The horizon was littered with ships. All over the sea and as far out as eye could reach the armada mottled the water.

Everybody aboard became excited at the prospect of being part of what looked like the first big American offensive of the war. Obviously, the warships were going to pave the way for a landing against some important enemy position.

I don't think many of us knew that our mission was to seize the Tulagi-Guadalcanal area. With all those ships before our eyes we were speculative about bigger game. Would we take a crack at Rabaul? Perhaps we would clean up Lae and Salamaua, in New Guinea, or pinch off the Solomons at Buka Passage, on the northern end of Bougainville Island. We were getting ready for something big, but we didn't know what, so we spent most of our time guessing.

Toward the end of July some idea of what this large force of carriers and transports was going to do in the South Pacific leaked out and gradually seeped down to the junior officers. As I got it from several sources, we had three separate tasks to be accomplished before our mission was completed. The first task had three phases.

The first phase was to consist of rehearsal landing exercise on an island. All aircraft squadrons and all warships—battleships, cruisers, and destroyers—were to take part. They would join in clearing the way for the Marines to make a landing on shore. Small bombs and service ammunition would be used by aircraft in this simulation.

The co-ordination of units in their practice landing operations was mapped out somewhat as follows. First, the stubby little Grumman fighters were to attack to destroy enemy aircraft, using 100-pound bombs to wipe out airfield installations and .50-caliber machine gun slugs to strafe planes on the ground and in the water. Then the Douglas Dauntless dive bombers would go in to put enemy shore batteries out of action. Next, the warships were to lay down a barrage on the beach under which the Marine raiders would start their landing.

The second phase of the first task was the actual occupation of the Tulagi-Guadalcanal area, and the third phase was the protection of our supply lines to the captured territory from the New Hebrides. I never was able to discover what the second and third tasks were.

On July 30 the landing exercises on the island were conducted according to plan. The torpedo planes were used that day as tactical scouts to protect the carrier forces from a real attack from the rear, while our own mock offensive was undertaken. We threaded our way in two plane sections through the rocky but densely wooded islands that were scattered about the sea and flew out over the spacious ocean beyond in search of enemy vessels, but found none. From the carrier, the island could be seen most of the day to the northwest. The operations were carried out successfully, and we steamed south.

There was something ludicrous to some of us in this huge armada's suddenly appearing from the ocean vastness and pouncing with all its strength upon one small island which we already owned. It convinced us that we could take these islands at least.

"I guess that will teach those Japs a lesson," Richey said as we retired that night.

Jaccard used to say that we were just fighting a Gilbert and Sullivan war anyway. To back his point he told us that an admiral had fallen in the water while disembarking from one carrier to attend a conference on another, then sloshed his way back to his cabin red-faced and spluttering, and refused to come out the remainder of the day.

Once one of the other carriers sent a plane over to our ship to borrow a crate of fresh eggs. They intended to have omelet for lunch, the pilot said, but didn't have quite enough eggs. The visitor was refused because we didn't have a big supply ourselves. It reminded us of housewives bickering over the back fence. That afternoon I asked Jaccard what sector he was searching, and he said, "Oh, my dear, I've given up that awful searching. It's so hard on the complexion! I must run over to Sarah's and borrow a cup of sugar. Poor George will be so disappointed if I don't bake him a cake for dinner tonight."

On another occasion our carrier became separated from the other two during the night. This often happens at sea in the war zone, where radio silence is in effect and the warships have no means of communicating with one another during darkness. The next day a fighter pilot from another carrier out looking for us winged in and dropped a message on our deck saying that he couldn't find us. He then signaled for a landing, and we took him aboard. He was chagrined enough when he discovered that he hadn't been able to tell his own carrier from another, but his humiliation was overwhelming when the air officer assigned two dive bombers to lead him like a lost child back to his own flat-top.

That night the war information bulletin, which was printed and distributed by the ship to all hands every day, contained this line at the bottom: "It's a wise bird that knows its own mother."

The war information bulletin often enclosed bits of poetry in order to drive a point home to pilots or ship's personnel.

One bit of doggerel which seemed to stick in the mind was a verse designed to keep our anti-aircraft gunners aware of the fact that a plane will fall if it's hit in the engine. It ran:

> If you shoot him in the prop
> You'll make the basket flop.

If you shoot him in the rudder
You'll only make him shudder.

Others were:

Tracers are red,
Incendiaries are blue.
We don't like Japs,
And we know what to do.

and

A strange old bird is the wise old owl,
His head on a swivel and a perpetual scowl,
Imitate him and you're sure to find
No Jap will surprise you from behind.

and

A thousand-pounder packs an awful sting
But unless it hits—it don't mean a thing.

A fighter pilot was sent to drop a message on another carrier one day after we left the islands, and when he returned he began to frisk around over the carrier while waiting for it to turn into the wind so he could land. He came up over the ramp at about 100 feet and started a slow roll off the starboard side. He almost made it but mushed down as he came out and hit the water not 100 yards from the ship. There was an explosion, a flash of fire and a puff of smoke, and the plane disintegrated and sank immediately. I looked out the port and could see only a circular patch of burning gas from the ruptured tanks marking the surface where the plane had struck.

Nobody criticized the pilot for making that slow roll. American fighter pilots are supposed to have enough steam in their breeches to try something out of the book once in a while. The fact that he didn't make it was his own business.

Willie Wileman commented shortly after that, "Well, I'm

convinced that the Airplane is here to stay, but I'm not so sure about the Pilot."

At least once a day aboard the carrier I used to stand on the ammunition shack forward of the island structure and watch the planes as they took off or landed. I looked at the aircraft as they rumbled up the deck and rose off the bow, and I could see the countenances of the pilots as they passed me. Many faces, like that of Buck Manfred, were stern and strong, intent and set on the job of getting off the carrier. Some showed more expression. Towheaded Micheel used to stick his tongue out and try to bite it off. Our Skipper, Charlie Jett, chewed gum viciously; others let their mouths fall open and were sensitive and watchful. A few had an apprehensive look. Ensign Jorgenson, veteran of the Marshall-Gilbert raid and the Coral Sea battle, whistled as though he were off to see his best girl. And Jerry Stablein, the big overgrown bear, always looked as though he were about to have a healthy bowel movement.

I must admit that in watching landings I used to like to see accidents, because they were exciting. But after a time, when too often a spectacular crash resulted in a friend's being hurt, I grew sick of this aspect of flying and was pleased to see a good landing.

Because only one plane can maneuver, land, or take off on the deck at one time the operation of carrier planes high-lights the performance of the individual pilot. All eyes on the flight deck are on one plane, and the pilot is in the limelight. Everybody sees and notes exactly what he does. If he skids in the groove or overthrottles before take-off and bounces his tail all hands are witness. This fact tends to make carrier activity a show, and each pilot senses this to some degree. For this reason, near the fly one officer at the spot are men who check each plane before take-off for wings locked, flaps down, prop low pitch, hook up, tail wheel unlocked, etc., in case the pilot becomes muddle-headed.

One day shortly before we went into the Solomons I had a forced landing aboard the carrier. I was just completing an exercise torpedo run on the ship when my motor began to cut out. It would cut out for a second or two and then catch again exactly as a Ford I once owned did when there was a clog in the fuel line. After circling the ship twice trying to make the plane run true by adjusting the controls, and having no success, I made an emergency pass on the starboard side with my hook down, which is the signal for a delayed forced landing. The ship did not clear the deck so I circled again and passed down the portside, which is the signal for an immediate forced landing circle. Only then did they swing her into the wind, and I got into the landing circle and began my approach. Coming up the groove as I got a "low" signal, I added throttle and the engine conked again astern of the ramp. It caught just in time, and the signal officer gave me the cut. The motor died as soon as I chopped the throttle. The mechs told me that there was a stoppage in the carburetor. The number of the plane was Tare 13.

I'm sure that if Jaccard heard me tell this he would give me the old "ace of the base" treatment which he gave all pilots who yapped about exploits in the air. Jaccard was always right there with a better one, which he made up on the moment. "There I was at 20,000 feet, on my back, over Rabaul, with three Zeros on my tail, all hell busting loose, and navigating within one degree," he would say, at the same time winging around the room with the palms of his hands.

About August 2 we were told officially that the mission of our force was to capture and defend the Guadalcanal-Tulagi area. In the days that followed until August 7, as our fleet slowly crept northward through the Coral Sea, the plans for the attack were outlined for us. Each unit knew beforehand exactly what it was to do, what targets it was to attack, and at what time. The operations plan was drawn up around "Dog Day" (August 7) and detailed down to the minute before and after H hour (for Tulagi) and zero hour (for Guadalcanal).

The carriers were to form the air support groups. Other groups included fire support groups of heavy and light cruisers and destroyers to shell the beach heads at Guadalcanal and Tulagi and screening groups of warships to protect the transports and carriers.

Roughly analyzed, the attack on Tulagi was to proceed somewhat as follows. On Dog Day before sunrise the fighters would buzz in to bomb airfields and strafe aircraft concentrations. They intended to stir up a big stink in general in an attempt to cause panic. If they knocked out the aircraft on the ground and in the harbors the whole job would be much easier.

Shortly before sunrise the fire support groups of warships would shell enemy objectives on the island. Then eighteen dive bombers from our carrier would go down on anti-aircraft emplacements, radio stations, fuel and ammunition dumps, airfields, and troop concentrations. The warships were to start lobbing shells again as soon as the dive bombers cleared. Then another group of "hawks" from the other carrier, this time accompanied by fighters, would dive to bomb and strafe. Finally, at H hour the toughest Marine raiders—the nation's front-line shock troops—would ground on Beach Blue on the little island. The transports from which they disembarked would be lying about five miles offshore, protected by the screening group.

The same plan, roughly speaking, was outlined for the Guadalcanal area, where Marines were to land on Beach Red at zero hour after support from sea and air.

Fortune was kind to the American force as it closed on the Solomons in the first days of August. The Japs were patrolling the approach to the island from the south by long-range bombers, and the command thought it more than likely that we would be picked up before we closed to within effective striking range. The anticipation was that the fight would start before Dog Day—as soon as the Japs discovered our fleet—and that we would have to slug our way in to a landing.

Evidently we were not spotted, however, or the Japs would surely have done something about it. On August 6 the force was blanketed by a large frontal area which covered its approach. Even so, there was a rumor that a torpedo narrowly missed the ship on the night before.

At sunset before Dog Day we were only eighty-five miles from Guadalcanal.

After supper that evening our air officer, Commander Crommelin, wound up the discussion on details of the attack and gave us some last-minute advice.

"Show no quarter," he said. "Don't hesitate to be absolutely ruthless. You can be sure you will receive the same treatment.

"For eight months now we have been on the defensive. Tomorrow the tide is going to turn."

The part the TBFs would play in the morrow's activities had not been fixed as yet. We would either be used as search planes or sit on the deck with torpedoes hung in our bomb bays ready to attack if enemy shipping was turned up.

I was in Hoot Gibson's room the night before Dog Day. His favorite tune at that time was "Blues in the Night." He said he would give a "hooey da hooey" just as he went into his first dive on the next day. I was to listen to see if I could pick him up on the air.

8

Zero Hour—Dog Day

BOOTS AND SADDLES, the trumpet call for flight quarters aboard a carrier, had us hurrying to our stations two hours before sunrise on August 7. The torpedo squadron ready room was located in the island structure, and not long after we settled in our chairs we heard the fighters kick over and start to warm up on the flight deck. About an hour before dawn the first fighter roared at open throttle and left fly one to race up the deck and leap into the air. The dive bombers, their propellers sounding a more metallic whine, took off soon after the fighters.

Meantime the torpedo pilots had been receiving their instructions. Eight Avengers were to be sent out on a 200-mile search in sectors north and west of the battle area to locate enemy surface craft. They were to be loaded with four 500-pound bombs apiece. Each plane would search a single sector by itself. The remaining six planes were ordered to stand by on the flight deck, loaded with torpedoes, ready to launch an attack if enemy warships were encountered. I was of this last group, but at the same time I was also a stand-by for search in case one of the regular planes was unable to take off.

That is what happened. One of the search TBFs developed engine trouble at the spot, and I was shot up from the hangar deck and waved off the carrier with a torpedo instead of bombs. The last instructions relayed to me by our squadron's leading chief were to drop the torpedo before I came back aboard. I had never landed aboard with a 2,000-pound torpedo slung in the belly, and I imagine the air officer did not want to risk plane and crew for the sake of saving a torpedo in case I didn't find anything to drop on.

I was in the air and headed out on the first leg of my search by seven o'clock. It was a beautiful morning, bright and clear. I could smell the vegetation from the land as I approached the Rossel Islands, the first group of small islands on my track, and soon I was over a thick, bright green jungle steaming in the early sun. Flocks of pure white birds fluttered from the treetops ahead of me, and once or twice I mistook the stream of their flight for smoke. From the air the only habitations visible were a few grass huts inland and red and white wooden plantation buildings along the shoreline.

I passed the Rossel Islands and was heading across the channel toward Santa Isabel when I saw the explosion of a bomb in Jerry Stablein's sector to my left. I put my nose on the column of smoke, checked my compass, and flew over to investigate. The smoke cleared away, but I kept my heading and soon spotted a small seventy-five-foot cargo vessel. I closed low on the water to take a look at them, and they began to fire at me with one or more small automatic weapons—probably a sub machine gun. I saw the splashes in front of me where the bullets hit the water and ricocheted. I turned past the ship's bow and told my gunner over the interphone to open fire with his .50-caliber turret gun. He answered that the gun was jammed. I tried my forward armament, which didn't fire either. I learned very quickly, however, that I had simply forgotten to charge it.

We left the cargo vessel and continued on our long search. I had decided to get the guns in operation on the leg out and then make another pass at the vessel on the way back. I also intended to drop my torpedo on this little boat if I didn't run across any bigger and more worth-while game in another part of the sector.

We flew on over the mountains of Santa Isabel, peeked into Rekata Bay, and then headed northward to Roncador Reef. This circular atoll has a passage on the south side of it, and we thought the Japs might be using the lagoon as an anchorage. The whole formation of the atoll was completely under water, about four feet deep, but it was visible from a distance by the wash of waves breaking over the shoal. There wasn't even a rowboat in the lagoon, and after circling it I turned southward again.

After we had recrossed Santa Isabel we began to hunt about for the small cargo vessel that had fired on us. We had some little difficulty in picking her up again but finally found her huddled in the midst of a rainstorm. We came in low on the water, and they opened fire on us long before we were in range. I watched the little spurts of water creeping closer and closer to me, and when they were just under the nose I jinked over and the gunner had to pick up my range again. It was pitiful in a way, I thought, for them to be opposing an armored warplane with one small-caliber machine gun. I dropped my torpedo at minimum range and flew on past the bow of the ship and pulled up. Looking back, I could see the wake of the pickle eating through the water about twenty feet ahead of the boat. I had led the vessel too much and missed.

After launching the torpedo I came back to strafe. I made several runs, each time coming in low on the sea and raking the deck with my forward gun, then pulling up in a wing over above the ship, allowing my turret gunner to dum his heavier slugs downward into the structure. We fired until most of our ammunition was gone. As I came in the second time I saw somebody jump overboard, and then when I passed just over the mast I glanced down and saw another crew member with black hair and a red shirt run and stumble under a canopy which shaded the deck. My gunner had the word by that time, and his tracers were looping into the vessel and pinking off the deck. My eyes were watering from the smell of gunpowder when we gave up the attack.

When I first went in to investigate this ship on the outbound leg, I didn't intend to molest it and wouldn't have if they hadn't fired on me first. Even later when I did open fire I felt a little timid, because I never had actually shot at anyone before, and either training or instinct made me feel that it was wrong.

On my first run I had my gun bearing squarely on the deck and was sluing it as I came in, for an interval of about six or seven seconds. I found myself squeezing the trigger hard and setting my jaw firmly. At first I mistook this reaction for the grim determination I had seen in the movies registered on the faces of pilots as they fired on the enemy, but I realized almost immediately that this wasn't the case. My manner was a result partly of making myself do something I didn't wholeheartedly want to do and partly of my effort to keep my guns bearing.

After my torpedo had missed I didn't feel sorry right away. My first thought was, what shall I do now, and my second the decision to strafe. I think I felt a little relieved also that sixteen or twenty men hadn't been blown to bits. I say this sincerely and not in an effort to whitewash my failure. I didn't begin to feel at fault about missing until I had returned to the ship and been kidded about it.

But my attempt to sink that small ship did make me a better combat pilot, I believe. In the first place, I never again got far from the carrier without test-firing all my guns. In the second place, I had overcome certain inherent mental and moral barriers. At first, when I thought of sending men to their death by slogging a torpedo into that vessel in a one-sided fight, and later, when I strafed and saw them scurrying for cover, I felt ashamed. But after I thought about it and realized that this was only a logical incident in a dirty war, I knew it wouldn't be so hard to do next time.

That afternoon I flew on intermediate air patrol in a sector within a radius of fifty miles of the carrier. I learned when I landed that evening that I had been almost shot down. Four of our fighters returning from the Tulagi area picked me up as an unidentified plane. I saw two of them on my starboard quarter above me and thought it was fine to have an escort but missed two more who had ducked in below me. The pilot of one of these planes told me that he had me within 100 yards, his eye on the sight and his finger on the trigger, when he caught sight of the star under the wing of my plane.

The first day's operations against the islands of Tulagi, Gavutu, and Tanambango in Gavutu Harbor and against Guadalcanal across the channel were evidently a complete success. Early in the day fighters put out of action all enemy patrol planes and Zeros in the immediate area, most of them on the ground. The Marines landed on Guadalcanal and were advancing toward Henderson Field. Tulagi was proving more difficult to storm but was expected to fall soon.

Enemy bombers which arrived from the north during the afternoon were routed by our fighters before they did any damage to our transports. Five Jap dive bombers which attempted to drop on warships near Guadalcanal were promptly shot down.

Harry March told of shooting down a "lame duck," a float plane which was just taking off. Harry slipped down on his tail, gave him one burst, and he hit the water and exploded in flames. Wileman was peeved, because he had been on combat air patrol over the ship and didn't even see an enemy bomber.

Hoot Gibson swore he gave his "hooey da hooey" yodel that day just before his first dive, but I never heard it over the air.

On the afternoon of August 8 I was assigned a 200-mile search to the northward. I passed around the southeastern tip of Guadalcanal, flew across the straits to the island of Malaita, and then headed seaward. At the end of my second leg I spotted a flying boat about ten miles away and opened the throttle to give chase. As soon as the patrol bomber saw my plane he turned his tail and dropped down on the water. It looked like a PBY, but I didn't see why he was running if it was. However, as soon as I came in from underneath and caught him I glimpsed the white star on the side of his nose. We waggled wings at each other and parted.

On my return leg I flew over Tulagi and took a look at the combat area from about 1,000 feet.

A big fire was sending up billows of white smoke on Tulagi Island, but otherwise it seemed relatively untouched. Gavutu and Tanambango islands, on the contrary, had been turned into red-earth pancakes in the water. A few houses were smoldering on each, but otherwise there wasn't a sign of activity. On Gavutu there was a large rectangle of white crosses planted in symmetrical rows.

In the harbor the warships and transports were still milling about. One transport had been hit and was smoking, a long funnel of smoke pouring out of one side of the deck. Behind Tulagi a destroyer was firing toward Guadalcanal.

After leaving Tulagi I abandoned my navigation and hopped over Guadalcanal and out to sea to the place where I thought the fleet was. If our carrier had been where it was supposed to be I would have seen it, but it was about thirty miles to the northeastward. Nevertheless, the fact that I hadn't navigated carefully made me lose confidence in my ability to find the ship. The area was choked with thick cumulus rain clouds. Sunset was due at six-eighteen, and at six o'clock it was begining to grow dark. Gradually I had to admit to myself that I didn't know where I was, that I was lost, and that night was falling fast. There was no radio silence that day, so at six-five I turned on my transmitter and asked the carrier to "spring me," in other words, to give me a course to fly back to the ship. I didn't hear an answer for about five minutes. Meantime, my gas was running low, it was getting darker minute by minute, and in that interval I was in the middle of a rain cloud at about 6,000 feet flying on instruments. I asked for a vector again, and my voice sounded loud and hollow in my ears. It began to get lonely up above the ocean that way in the midst of a storm, not being able to see anything.

I took my eyes off the instruments for a moment and turned to Deitsch, the bombardier, who was in the second seat. His face was scared and set. I smiled at him.

I had almost abandoned hope of reaching the carrier and was heading northward toward Guadalcanal in order to be near an island if I had to crash-land in the water. I thought by chance I might be able to fly around the island to Lunga (Henderson) Field. Then I heard from the ship, "Mears in Eight, steer one two zero. Mears in Eight, steer one two zero."

Whew! My worries were over if my gas held. I came in on the course they gave me, broke out of the clouds all of a sudden, and saw the bulk of one of the other carriers beneath me. I dove for her, got beneath the ceiling, and then saw my own carrier about five miles eastward. It was dark by then. The carrier turned into the wind, and I came barreling over the ramp at ninety knots, trying to get aboard. The signal officer gave me a wave-off for being too fast, and I settled down. On the next approach the wands looked good, spelling a "Roger" all the way, until the cut. I was aboard, and in my tanks was enough gas for three minutes more of flight.

"They told me you were missing," Gibson said, "but I wasn't worried. You've got just enough dumb luck to fly over the carrier in the dark without knowing it and catch your hook in a wire." I guess he was about right.

That night the carriers retired on a southeasterly course away from the combat area.

9

The Battle of Stewart Island

AFTER THE OFFENSIVE of August 7 and 8 our carrier forces began a game of ticktacktoe with the Japs which lasted until August 24, when we clashed head on again in one of those rugged carrier-versus-carrier slugging matches. When two opposing carrier forces meet both are in for trouble, since it is seldom that one carrier can discover and attack another without being discovered itself. Both usually have almost the same scouting range. Often the two opposing attack groups will pass each other in the air on the way to their separate objectives.

On our way southward we heard rumors of an ever-increasing concentration of Jap air power and naval strength in the Rabaul-Solomon area.

We received reports of enemy bombing attacks on our ships in Tulagi Harbor and on Lunga Field. Four of our cruisers were said to have been sunk in a night naval engagement off Savo Island.

On August 12 Hoot Gibson and Jerry Richey took off just at dawn and almost immediately surprised a submarine lying on the surface about twenty miles ahead of the carrier. Gib said it was more accurate to say the submarine surprised him. He almost spun in when he first saw it, he laughed, but managed to make a run on it immediately and drop a 500-pound bomb within fifty feet of it. Richey followed him in and shook the sub by placing his egg within twenty feet of the hull. Thereafter it lay on the surface for five or six minutes in a down-by-the-bow attitude while both planes made repeated strafing attacks, firing their fifties forward and their free guns aft. Richey said he saw some Japs lying on the deck and others struggling in the water. Finally the Jap prowler settled below the surface, still in a down-by-the-bow attitude but making no apparent headway. Both Gibson and Richey received official commendation for their neat disposal of the raider.

When our carrier forces had fueled they started a sprint northward again in an effort to intercept Jap surface forces preparing to attack Guadalcanal, but the contact with these enemy units remained undeveloped and we slowed to fifteen knots.

After August 20 evidences of the enemy's presence became more and more numerous, and it became apparent that a conflict of some sort was brewing.

On August 21, 22 and 23 contact was made with an enemy body of two heavy cruisers, three destroyers, and four transports.

Two enemy submarines were picked up and bombed by our search planes on August 23. That same evening and the next morning contact was made with a Jap carrier force to the north of us. This is what we had been waiting for.

On the afternoon of the twenty-fourth TBFs and SBDs of our carrier took off to make an extensive 250-mile search in the area north of the Solomons to find the enemy flat-top. The *Wasp* had gone southward to fuel the night before, but attack groups on our carrier and on the other carrier in our force waited on deck to launch as soon as word of contact was radioed back.

Charlie Jett, skipper of our squadron, was the first to sight the enemy. At about two-thirty he and Ensign Bye (whom we called the "Dead-End Kid" for his habit of telling foul jokes out of the side of his mouth) picked up a small carrier of the *Ryujo* class, keyed back the contact message, and then attacked. They made a horizontal bombing run at 12,000 feet but claimed no hits.

At about three-thirty Bomron Ray Davis, the skipper of Bombing Six, ran across another enemy force of two large carriers guarded by a screening force of cruisers and destroyers stretching over the ocean for forty miles. They reported over the air and attacked, scoring two hits on one of the carriers.

I was on the afternoon search flying wing on Weasel Weissenborn. We heard some muttering over the air at one time but couldn't make it out. The mere fact that radio silence had been broken ought to have put us on the alert, but we flew on back toward our carrier fat and happy. At five fifteen we reached the ship, made our recognition signal, and started to approach the carrier. I looked over and saw a cruiser which was smoking. I thought it looked as though it had been hit and that our force had been attacked while we were gone.

All of a sudden a terrific barrage of A.A. fire burst from all the ships in the force. The battleship accompanying our carrier lit up like a Christmas tree. Black and white puffs of smoke covered the late afternoon sky. Our ships began to turn, and their wakes curved boiling out behind them.

I looked up and saw three Jap dive bombers, one behind the other, diving on our carrier. They seemed to be coming down very slowly. It was like pictures I'd seen of the Pearl Harbor raid.

I heard on the air: "All friendly planes keep clear during the attack." Weasel and I were circling just outside of our dispositon at the time, watching the show. I almost forgot to fly the plane, I got so interested in what was going on.

I saw a mass of flame—a plane burning fiercely—flutter down like a butterfly and kiss the water. Shrapnel was falling in patches on the ocean like heavy rain. Bombs struck the sea near us and made dirty brown circles in the water. The cruiser I thought hit was only smoking from the volume of anti-aircraft fire it was throwing up.

Over the radio came the word: "SBDs attack the torpedo planes." This was also our meat, I decided, and left Weissenborn to head in toward our carrier. On the way in I met two Jap dive bombers coming out. I had never seen a Jap plane at close quarters before, and I thought they were Zeros. Yipe! I banked to get my turret gun bearing and at the same time to return to join Weasel again. They chased me back into formation—Weasel had taken a wing on the skipper by that time—and then one of the Jap planes left for home.

The other peeled off and began to make runs on us. We were flying formation in a three-plane section close to the water in a left turn. I watched, fascinated, as he closed on us the first time. I could see his brownish white wings—the camouflage looked more than anything like a poor paint job—with red circles on them. As he headed toward us he opened fire, and two long, yellowish streamers of smoke came out of his nose. It seemed as though he were aiming straight at me, and I remember thinking, "Jesus, I don't want him to shoot me," in just these words. As he came overhead and started to pull up I whipped off and shot at him with my little forward popgun. "Well, I'll be damned," I thought, "I'm shooting at a Zero." I still believed it was a Zero. My tracers made me think I was hitting him, but he didn't fall.

He made seven runs on us all together. We had our three .50-caliber turret guns on him all the time, but he didn't go down. It was rather ridiculous, in a way, everybody firing like mad and nobody getting hurt.

After the attack we circled the carrier, watching the fire crews struggling with the first aft on the flight deck. There were Jett, Weissonborn, Bye, Weis and myself. Flying on our skipper, I saw him lift his canteen to his mouth and tilt his head back to drain it. I felt suddenly thirsty myself.

Johnny Myers soon joined us in the circle. His plane was all shot to hell, the tail section half gone, but it was still in the air. He grinned at me and put his fingers to the corners of his eyes—the slant-eye Jap sign.

At six-fifteen we received word to jettison our bombs and land. I left the formation, flew out about five miles, dropped my two 500-pound bombs, felt the whoof of the explosion under the plane, and returned to land. There were no planes in our landing circle, so I joined on plane T-8 around the other carrier. Bob Divine was flying it. I waved to him, then noticed they were landing on our carrier again, so I went back and got aboard my own ship.

When I landed half the flight deck aft was blown up by a bomb hit. I came in on the white paddles, and it was almost dark when I caught the wire. The plane handler who taxied me up the deck had a bandage around his head under his helmet. Everybody looked tired.

In the ready room we heard the story of the bombing. There had been no general alarm. The attack came just as the last torpedo plane in our attack group left the deck, and the first indication those in the ready room had was the pounding of the carrier's A.A. guns.

They were all playing off a cribbage tournament at the time, and Bill Esders says the cards and cribbage boards flew all over the ready room as they kicked the chairs out of the way and lay down on the floor. One of the A-V (S) officers was vainly trying to jam a rubber life jacket over his head with his helmet on, and another was wringing his hands. When I got aboard they all looked as though they'd been up for three days. From what I am told being aboard a ship when it is a bombing target is one of the most terrifying experiences there is. There are no fox holes on a carrier.

Immediately after the attack the steering apparatus suddenly broke down, and the carrier veered into a violent turn and almost rammed a destroyer. The ship ran in circles for a time, until the rudder was put in action again.

Everybody needed a cigarette badly, but even this comfort was denied them, for the ship was still afire and no smoking was the order.

Only four torpedo planes were aboard. Weissenborn said he saw Bye leave the formation and go in the water. Then I remembered seeing a plane veer off and also recalled noticing three rubber boats in the water ahead of the carrier.

Johnny Myers got aboard the other carrier.

Bingaman and Corl were missing. Two days later we heard that Bingaman had landed near Stewart Island and was aboard a destroyer. Nothing was ever heard of Corl, but since he was flying wing on Johnny Myers, who was so badly shot up, it was assumed he was knocked into the water by enemy planes.

I saw Jaccard, and he told me Gibson was missing. (He had landed in the water and was later picked up by a destroyer.) Many other pilots we knew were not there, for several reasons. For one thing, just before the bombing we had sent out an attack group of dive bombers and torpedo planes. Other pilots had set their planes in the water when they ran out of gas, still others were aboard the other carriers, and a few had been shot down. At the time we didn't know which was which.

Despite the situation, we had a good dinner in the wardroom that evening and afterwards went to survey by moonlight the damage done by Jap bombs.

At about ten o'clock that night our attack group of six TBFs returned to the carrier. The moon was obscured by clouds. They circled, and we climbed up on the ammunition shack to see the night landings. Baker came aboard first. A good landing. Then Holley came up the groove, cut his gun, and floated out of the blackness until his plane appeared in clear outline over the deck, large and menacing and high above the ship. He kept floating, and we who were watching knew he was flying in to certain disaster. It was a sickening sight. He crashed headlong into the crane at the after end of the island structure, catching one wing near the fuselage and crumpling it. The plane rolled over and died on deck like a huge prehistoric bird with the other wing looming into the night sky. The crash looked like a bad one. By some miracle, however, no one was hurt.

The other four planes of the attack group landed on the other carrier instead of waiting for the deck crew to clear the wreckage from our deck.

The next morning Dick and I went out on the flight deck to view the damage by daylight. One 300-pound bomb had struck and exploded instantaneously on the starboard side near the second elevator. The hole which it had blown in the deck was covered by sheets of metal. There were shrapnel holes in the deck and in the pom-pom gun mounts near by. No casualties were apparent.

Near the after elevator there were two 500-pound hits. Both had made little foot-in-diameter holes as they pierced the deck, and both had exploded below, one in the chief's quarters. I looked through the hole and could see men working knee deep in water and debris on the steering apparatus far below.

One of the bombs had gone through an ammunition room below the flight deck and exploded it in passing. This powder

THE BATTLE OF STEWART ISLAND   121

room blew up and out, ballooning the flight deck and wiping out an entire gun gallery of two 5-inch guns on the starboard side.

Sailors' bodies were still in the gun gallery. Most of the men died from the concussion and then were roasted. The majority of the bodies were in one piece. They were blackened but not burned or withered, and they looked like iron statues of men, their limbs smooth and whole, their heads rounded with no hair. The faces were undistinguishable, but in almost every case the lips were drawn back in a wizened grin giving the men the expression of rodents.

The postures seemed either strangely normal or frankly grotesque. One gun pointer was still in his seat leaning on his sight with one arm. He looked as though a sculptor had created him. His body was nicely proportioned, the buttocks were rounded, there was no hair anywhere. Other iron men were lying outstretched, face up or down. Two or three lying face up were shielding themselves with their arms bent at the elbows and their hands before their faces. One, who was not burned so badly, had his chest thrown out, his head way back, and his hands clenched.

The blackened bodies did not appear as shocking as those only partially roasted. They looked more human in their distortion.

All together, there were about 100 dead. Services were held on August 26. One body was committed to the sea near the second elevator on the hangar deck, where the services were held. The others were thrown over the fantail. All the remains were enclosed in canvas sacks "properly enshrouded," the minister said. Four sailors upended a pantry board affair on which the symbolic body lay, and it slid from under the American flag into the ocean. Then the band played taps, the Marine guard gave present arms, and we saluted.

The bodies on the fantail were dumped off at the same time.

Our ship was the only one damaged in the battle, as far as I know, and it was still able to carry on flight operations if need be. Our plane losses were not immediately apparent, and I never was able to learn the exact figures. However, I'm sure they did not compare with those of the Japs. More than fifty Jap aircraft were shot down by A.A. fire or fighter-patrol on the attack on our flat-tops alone. One Nip torpedo squadron of eight planes was intercepted sixty miles from our carrier and dumped in the water.

The other carrier with us was over the horizon while we were being bombed. Attack groups had taken off from her deck to strike at the Jap surface forces during the middle of the afternoon.

Torpedo Eight, based aboard her, had gone out in two sections to strike the enemy. Seven torpedo planes, under the lead of Lieutenant Bruce Harwood, the executive officer, attacked the *Ryujo* and set her afire with the aid of bombing squadrons. They also hit a cruiser on the same sally. Larsen took a group of five planes in to strike another group of eighteen enemy cruisers and destroyers, and his flight was given credit for hitting a cruiser.

As in the Battle of Midway, I could not be sure of the exact results, but from all reports we seemed to have come out with a considerable edge in this reciprocal pounding by air.

On the evening of August 26 our skipper called together the eight pilots in our squadron who were left on the carrier and told us that five would fly the remaining planes off the deck in the morning. We were to proceed to a field in the New Hebrides to fill in as carrier replacements. The ship was bound for port to be repaired. The skipper himself and Esders, Engel, Holley, and myself were to go. The planes of Bombing Six were leaving with us.

The next morning we settled in our cockpits, the breeze in our faces, the motion of the sea beneath us, waiting to take off. Many old-timers of the ship were leaving her today, most of them never to see her again, so the occasion was one of farewell. The air officer spoke over the amplifier: "This is the air officer speaking. Give 'em hell." Then the assistant air officer spoke: "This is the assistant air officer speaking. Stand by to start engines." There would be no sentimental guff from him. Everybody laughed.

I was the first torpedo pilot to take off. We were all heavily overloaded with a torpedo and more than 1,000 pounds of ordnance and personal gear. The fly one officer gave me the thumbs-up signal for good luck, smiled, and waved me off. I made a straight run at full throttle down the deck, but even so I settled about twenty feet off the bow. Engel and Esders followed. We circled and waited for Jett and Holley.

We watched the skipper move up the deck. He was more heavily loaded than any of us and never got his tail up until just before he slid over the bow. He almost made it, but one wing caught the water and spilled him. Holley took off a short time later. His motor was not giving full power, and he was coming down the back stretch trying to get aboard again when he spun in. All the occupants of both planes were rescued by the guard destroyer.

We saw both the planes go in and circled down to see that the personnel were still afloat. The Navy loses a lot of planes to the sea. It can't be helped. What we ourselves were worried about, once we saw that the boys had only got a wetting, were our pay accounts, which were in the skipper's plane. Unless we ran across the carrier again we would not be paid for months.

The remaining three of us flew on into the New Hebrides with the bombing squadron according to our orders. We landed on a dusty, narrow field bordered by jungle and tied down our planes. That evening we went into the little French town near by on the bay and looked for something to drink. The only place we could find to get anything at all was a dirty French restaurant run by a sixteen-year-old boy named François. François was somewhat of a tyrant and conscious of his power as holder of the beer and wine monopoly on the island. We were able to buy enough wine to get drunk on only after we had flattered him about his ability to snare the girls and cheat at cards. When we had lapped up enough of the gritty red wine he served us Jaccard, Engel, and I wandered outside into the moonlight. It was such a lovely night and we were so exhilarated by the wine that we thought we'd like to take a trip around the island. We stole an army jeep and charged over all the roads available until we were tired enough to go to bed.

I said good-by to Jaccard a week later on a narrow jungle path as he was going to pack his things, preparatory to flying southward. "I'll see you in a couple of weeks, Ears," he said, we shook hands, and parted.

Bill Esders, Larry Engel and I flew north to join Torpedo Squadron Eight in another jungle camp of the New Hebrides, We sensed that our destination was Guadalcanal.

I had known most of the men in Larsen's detachment of Torpedo Eight for a short time after Midway. "Andy" Divine had remained with the squadron when I transferred to Torpedo Three, and he and Bert Earnest were down at the strip of field in the jungle to meet us. When we got to the squadron camp on the hill behind the field, we found the other members of Torpedo Eight busy clearing away brush and burning it, pitching their tents and setting up cots covered with mosquito netting. They had been set ashore from a carrier only a short time ago and were prepared to make themselves as comfortable as possible in the hot and humid forest.

In the month that followed before we went to Guadalcanal, Bill Esders, an experienced enlisted pilot who was a wizard with the pasteboards, and Larry Engel, a clean-cut lad from Oregon, and I helped the others improve on the camp. We dug our own latrine, and we built our own shower by pulling two oil barrels full of water on top of a log stand we had erected. Lieutenant Benny Grosscup, who was one of the "eleven iron men" of the Yale football team which beat Princeton in 1934 with no substitutions, directed these activities. "Bum Dope" Benny, as we called him, was our intelligence officer and continually was dishing out depressing news which he got from the griddle, as he said, at staff headquarters. "It looks like a big mix coming up. Sixty Jap warships just left Truk headed southward," he would warn us, or he would tell us that "this place is next on the Japs' list."

There were two other Yale A-V (S) officers in the squadron, Lieutenant George Flinn ("The Admiral"), who directed the paper work of Torpedo Eight with meticulous efficiency, and DeWitt Peterkin, Jr., the engineering officer who, with the engineering chief, Hammond, was responsible for keeping most of the planes in the air most of the time.

The pilots of the squadron were Jack Barnum (Barney), a

small, energetic, heady flier who used to tease Ed Hanson (Hanse) into crying because he missed his girl Joyce after a few beers; easygoing "Smiley" Morgan; "Dirty John" Taurman, a quiet, good-looking boy who was later lost; "Bugger" Ries, who could always find something earthly to laugh at; Bob Evarts, Hanse's right-hand companion; Grady, of the cow-brown eyes; Aaron Katz, Larsen's anathema; Bruce Harwood, the executive officer; red-haired, talkative Ben Doggett, later killed; Dye, Divine, Earnest, and, of course, Larsen, the commanding officer.

It was while I was in this jungle camp that I got news of Jaccard's death aboard the *Wasp*. Jake had gone aboard her shortly after I left him. When she was torpedoed he was sound asleep in his bunk, and he went down with the ship. If he'd been in a plane I don't think they ever would have nailed him. Somehow, I didn't think it was possible for him to be killed anyway, but, as he would put it, *"C'est la guerre, c'est la vie, c'est l'amour."*

10

From Henderson Field

THE FLIERS OF Torpedo Squadron Eight crowded around Buck Manfred, who had just been flown out of Guadalcanal.

When I had seen Buck aboard the carrier three weeks before, he was good-looking and tall, with dark wavy hair and a healthy, smiling face. In fact, I had always thought of him as a walking recruiting poster for the navy air arm. Now he looked like a worn-out bum. His eyes were prominent and circled, he was thin as a bunch of sticks, his clothes were filthy, and he needed a shave.

He was giving us the word on Guadalcanal. He was dead tired, but we urged him to tell us what was happening before he took a shower and went to bed.

"Here's the deal," he said. "In daylight, our fighters are breaking up the bombers and routing the Zeros so that many Japs are shot down and others jettison their bombs and run.

"But at night, when we don't dare turn on the field lights to allow our planes to take off, the Japs bring one or two cruisers into the harbor and let go with their 8-inch guns.

"Jap planes circle over the field at night and drop flares to light the way for their bombs," Buck told us. "During the day the Japs fire at our planes entering the landing circle, after they return from attacks on enemy warships." The pilots were flying six to eight hours a day on scouting missions or attacks, and being bombed and shelled day and night on the ground. In addition, they were living on inferior food, which

126

included captured Jap fish and rice, and most of them had dysentery, if not malaria.

We were interested in getting the dope, because six members of our squadron had flown up there five days ago, and the rest of us expected to go up soon.

Three days after talking to Buck six of us flew our Grumman Avenger torpedo planes to Henderson Field, and I had my first look at Guadalcanal. It was an in-and-out trip, as we were merely ferrying torpedoes for the others to use.

As we approached the harbor I saw several warships under way. I spotted one of cruiser size, with an inverted-Y, or double, stack, which I knew was not one of ours and certainly looked like a Jap. I thought we would be making an attack before we got to the field. But the ship was an Australian cruiser, and we proceeded to make a landing.

Henderson Field was much larger and cleaner of jungle around its edges than I had imagined it. Nobody shot at us in the landing circle. We landed about two hours before sunset on a solid field. The first thing I noticed were the innumerable bomb craters and the junks of planes all around the strip. There wasn't a flyable plane in sight. I learned later that they were dispersed in another area.

Guadalcanal is such a beautiful place naturally that it is hard to associate it with the brutalities of war. When we arrived the boys took us down to the beach, and we looked across the golden sea at the islands of Florida, fringed by the distant outline of Malaita. At sunset we stood near the field on the edge of Lever Brothers Cocoanut Grove and watched the magic cloud colors above the mountains to the west.

Bert Earnest and Ferrier got together while we were there and began to talk over their flight from Midway. They both had great trust in one another, having come through that ordeal together. Bert asked me if he couldn't have Ferrier back, since he needed a good man in the turret while he was operating from the island, and as long as I was returning to the New Hebrides and didn't need a gunner I let Bert have him.

That night three of us who had never been there before were sleeping in the same tent. It was raining. About midnight we were awakened by someone scampering past who yelled, "Hit your fox holes!"

We weren't going to get wet for nothing, and as far as we could see there wasn't anything happening. So we stayed in our cots. Then we saw a glitter in the sky to the northward and soon heard an explosion not too far away.

"Let's not be stupid about this," said one of the boys, Aaron Katz.

"I think you've got something there," answered the other, Larry Engel; and all together we stumbled out of the tent into what we thought was our fox hole. It was occupied, and so was the next one (by men who already had fallen asleep there). We finally found a shallow and uncovered trench into which we squeezed, with arms and legs sticking out. A sub was lobbing shells at us.

Nothing spectacular happened, and we went back to bed. The next morning I left Guadalcanal thinking that the story of the place was exaggerated. Later I learned to have more respect for its dangers, and I became particularly adept at jumping into fox holes before I left the island. I took a great deal of pride in the fact that, given a glitter of light on the horizon, I could be out of my bunk and into the nearest fox hole first, with a helmet over my head before the shell exploded.

On October 1 Ensign Bob Evarts and I returned to Guadalcanal in a Flying Fortress. When we arrived we learned that five of our torpedo planes were out on an attack against four destroyers near Gizo, a small island in the New Georgia group. At that time, Lieutenant Bruce Harwood, executive officer of the squadron, had replaced Lieutenant H. H. Larsen, squadron commander, who was the first to come to Guadalcanal, as the leader of our group of torpedo planes on the island. Bruce was a tall veteran, slow of movement, gruff but generous, and a brilliant leader.

Harwood and Bob Ries landed about nine o'clock. Ries came into our tent with a long face and reported that our other three planes were lost. The pilots were Engel, Divine, and Dye. They failed to rendezvous on Harwood after the attack, probably because Harwood's radio wouldn't work and his lights were out. We turned in late that night and dove into fox holes early in the morning when a lone Jap plane droned over and bombed us.

After sunrise I took off and circled the island on a three-hour search for the lost pilots but didn't spot them. On the way I saw the wrecks of several Jap bombers and Zeros that had been shot down and one Grumman Wildcat scattered on the beach. The next day we received word that all three of the lost pilots from our squadron, with their crews, had been picked up and were aboard a destroyer.

A new gunner, George Hicks, was assigned to me when I reached Guadalcanal to stay. Hicks was formerly Grady's gunner, but Grady had fallen off a rapidly moving truck during an air raid and sprained his wrist and twisted his knee. Hicks was quick and watchful in the air, and I was pleased to get him.

At twelve-fifteen we had an air-raid alarm while at lunch and drove bouncing in a truck down to the beach. I finished my coffee on the way.

There we stood by our fox holes and watched our fighters tangle with a flight of Zeros that came in from the north. The flight was over the sea and mostly obscured by fluffy white clouds. But we often saw the vapor trails of fighters and followed them down until we saw the tiny black crosses of planes dog-fighting. We watched them zooming, twisting, and circling in the sky and heard the sudden chug-chug-chug which indicated that our fighters were firing their fifties.

One Zero dropped from the blue and made a pass at one of our dive bombers, which was flying at low altitude on anti-sub patrol for two of our ships in the channel. Then he did a loop and flew off westward. The Japs love to stunt their very maneuverable planes, and they often do so even in the midst of combat. Such an expression of exhilaration probably cost this Zero pilot his life, however, for as he was executing his loop our fighters caught sight of him. Four of them streamed down on him, and he dropped seaward as though out of control. Another trick. He leveled off just before he hit the water. But three more of our fighters came in on top of him and polished him off.

The next day I went on my first attack. In the late afternoon three Grumman Avenger torpedo planes and seven

Douglas Dauntless dive bombers took off to hit a cruiser and two destroyers, reported 150 miles westward of the "slot." I was loaded with four 500-pound bombs on this occasion, instead of a torpedo.

After the three torpedo planes had made their rendezvous and headed northwest we heard a pilot in a plane near Henderson Field telling the control tower not to send us in without fighter protection. "It's suicide, repeat, suicide," he said, "to send those planes in without fighters." "There are fifteen Zeros in the vicinity," he reported, and he kept insisting that control call us back. Finally, somebody picked up a mike and told him to "shut up."

At that time we three torpedo planes were up ahead, and the dive bombers or fighters were nowhere in sight. I was very nervous and felt as though I'd like to get up and walk around in the cockpit. The idea of making a glorious suicidal attack didn't thrill me a great deal. The only thing I could do, however, was try hard to think what maneuvers I would make if Zeros attacked. I checked to see that my guns were loaded and charged and that my bombs were armed. I told my bomber to remind me to open my bomb doors when I started to dive.

Evarts, who was leading the flight, finally circled, and the dive bombers caught us. There were no fighters.

We caught sight of the ships at about five-thirty, much sooner than we had expected. They were in a line, with one destroyer leading and one trailing the cruiser. From our altitude I couldn't have determined whether they were Japanese or American ships without a more studied look to pick out details. I knew they were warships, however, by their trim, solid lines and could tell the difference between the cruiser and the destroyer by the difference in size. The cruiser already had been hit and was smoking. The ships began to turn, and we flew around them to get in the sun. My turret gunner reported two float-type biplanes below us, and I saw four more ascending as we circled. There were no Zeros, and since the Jap biplane, while maneuverable, is not fast, I was much relieved.

The dive bombers dove first on the cruiser, from about 9,000 feet, and I could see their bombs falling all over the water but not hitting. Ries picked out a destroyer and dove on it, scoring two near misses. He then battled his way up against the biplanes and dropped the other two bombs.

Meanwhile, Evarts went in on the cruiser ahead of me, and I watched him dive as I glided down to get into position. I saw a near miss off the stern of the cruiser as I pushed into about a sixty-degree dive.

Dust which had settled in the cockpit on the field almost blinded me for an instant, and I couldn't get my eye on the sight. On this attack I was not flying my own plane, which Deitsch always kept clean, and I remembered thinking at the time, "Damn it, I wish Deitsch had gotten ahold of this plane before we took off." Finally the dust cleared, and I saw the smoke of the cruiser through it. I didn't have time for any other idle thoughts on the way down. I was intent on fixing my point of aim—the bow of the big cruiser below me. I pressed the bomb release three times and pulled up. I glanced at my altimeter. I was at 2,000 feet.

Close to port I saw a float biplane closing on us, and I kicked into a turn away from him. Then I felt the vibration of the turret gun firing, and Hicks told me over the interphone that he had shot him down. About the same time I heard over the air: "Give Mears credit for a hit." Later Hicks told me he had seen one of the bombs hit in a flash fire and smoke just behind the ugly inverted-Y stack.

I circled on down past a destroyer ahead of the cruiser, at about fifteen hundred feet, trying to make up my mind what to bomb next. The destroyer was firing broadsides at me, but missing. I wheeled down past the cruiser, thinking I would climb through his smoke in the rear and drop one from low altitude on the deck. At the time I thought I had only one bomb left. Actually, I had two.

We were only 800 yards from the cruiser, and Hicks was strafing the deck. As we went past they were firing at us, and I could see the bullets sprinkling like rain. Suddenly they found our range, and I could see tracers looping into us. Then I felt a blow as though something had slapped us on the tail.

Hicks cried, "Mr. Mears! Deitsch has been hit! I think we are hit badly! Let's get the hell out of here!" I turned and fled along the water. The Japs kept firing at me until I was about a mile away, and I saw the ack-ack bursting in the water ahead. When we were clear I told Hicks to go down and help Deitsch. He said Deitsch was very badly hurt.

I set course for Guadalcanal and opened her out to over 200 knots but flew low on the water so that if we crashed suddenly we'd have a better chance. My gunner told me we'd have to hurry to save Deitsch; but I had already determined to return, both on Deitsch's account and because I didn't know how badly the plane was damaged.

I radioed control that I had a wounded man in my plane. I got in just at twilight, after making 100 miles in forty minutes, and we rushed Deitsch to the hospital. Deitsch was hit in the right of his head, where there was a little round hole the size of a nickel. He was breathing easily, but he was cold and wan.

The next day I went to see Deitsch in the hospital. He was lying in the operating shack, in the middle of the room, in a semiconscious condition, pale and yellow, his eyes wandering about but showing no recognition. The doctor said he had three pieces of shrapnel in his brain and gave him little chance to live. However, the last I heard from him, a month later, he was still fighting for life and improving.

Just before we had taken off on that attack I had misplaced my gloves and asked Deitsch if he'd seen them. I evidently seemed distressed about it, for he said, "What's the matter? Are you superstitious about wearing gloves?"

"Yeah, a little," I replied.

"Then you can take mine," he said, "I'm not superstitious."

I was wearing his gloves when he got hit.

The engineers who looked at the plane next day found only three control wires holding the flipper and three the rudder. There was a hole you could put your head through where a 20-millimeter shell had hit the bomber's compartment and exploded inside, and perhaps twenty other holes in the tail of the fuselage, made by explosive bullets.

Four of our torpedo planes took off next morning to track down the cruisers and destroyers. They found the ships 150 miles up the channel and attacked. They claimed two torpedo hits on the cruiser.

If there was any pattern to the conflict between our planes on Guadalcanal and Jap planes and ships coming down the "groove" (the channel between the islands), it went something like this:

The Grumman Wildcat fighters and the Douglas Dauntless dive bombers were the backbone of our defensive and offensive power. The few torpedo planes that we had were an added deadly threat on the attack. There were no army planes on the field at that time, except a few P-39s used for strafing Jap ground positions. B-17s used the field as a stopover on the haul from the New Hebrides to Jap positions in the northern Solomons.

Every morning we sent out a scouting flight in an arc about Henderson Field. Usually these planes didn't find anything, unless it was a Jap force of cruisers and destroyers which had succeeded in breaking through to Guadalcanal the night before and was retreating.

At noon it was the Japs' turn and silver-winged bombers, between fifteen and thirty-five of them, accompanied by playful Zeros, flew in perfect formation over the field. Our Wildcats were up to meet them. Sometimes they found the Jap bombers and knocked them all out of the sky, and at others we watched their formation come over and leave unmolested.

Pilots who were not flying usually were on stand-by. They lolled around the ready tent in the middle of the field, reading, talking, smoking, watching the reports come in, and trying to keep out of the sun. In case of an air raid they scurried to their planes or rode to the safety of the beach. Upon "condition yellow," which meant that a raid was expected in forty-five minutes and which was indicated by raising a white flag, the fighter pilots would take off, and the scramble pilots—those who flew the other planes on the field to a designated rendezvous point to save them from bombs—followed. Upon "condition red," which meant enemy planes overhead in ten minutes and which was indicated by a black flag, the last stragglers left the field for safety in fox holes.

On the beach everybody stood by their fox holes and popped into them when they heard the first whistle of bombs overhead. The irregular whistle grows louder and louder, like the stirring of wind in the trees, until the bomb dumps—"whoom." A person who has never before heard that "whi-whi-whi-whi" of a bomb descending must inevitably think, "This is it," because the sound is much louder than would be expected.

The large Jap pagoda, which for two months after the Marines took Guadalcanal stood in the middle of the field, was the center of the target for the Japs, and yet it was never touched by a bomb. The Americans used it as their administration building, and the commanding general had his headquarters there. It was destroyed, finally, by Jap shellfire in the middle of October.

In the afternoon every day we sent out another scouting flight. They usually would discover the "Tokyo express coming down Broadway," or, in other words, the force of cruisers and destroyers which almost daily came down the channel in an effort to land troops and supplies or to shell us. If our air attack groups didn't stop them, they got through and accomplished that objective, unless they were surprised by American surface ships after dark—and this happened several times.

Pilots of the attack group on stand-by in the afternoon as a rule were nervous until the afternoon scouting flight made contact. They smoked and fidgeted more than the others. What they wanted to know all afternoon was "how many today." If two destroyers were coming down, it wasn't so bad; but if four cruisers and eight destroyers were "in the slot," it could be a dangerous mission.

The attack group almost invariably returned after dark, and then the Japs took over again. A lone bombing plane, which we called "Washing-Machine Charlie" and sometimes "Worry Willy," began to thrum over the field at about eight-thirty and drop flares and bombs. If any person showed a light during these times he was asking for a bullet. One private in our area shot at every flashlight or cigarette glow he could see, until we caught him. Our fox holes were our best friends in the darkness, and during the day we dug them deeper and made them stronger and more elaborate.

The food that we had when we first got to Guadalcanal

was terrible. We were eating at a transients' mess at the southwest corner of the field. For breakfast we had cereal, or rather gruel, with a limited amount of thin milk and sugar, and coffee. Lunch was crackers—a hard biscuit cracker—or a blob of boiled fish and coffee. Dinner was more substantial, with two dishes, usually an almost meatless stew and canned fruit, and coffee. Coffee is what kept us alive, I'm sure. Even if we were hungry enough to eat this fare we often had to run for the beach to avoid a noon air raid just as it was time for lunch, or we had to take off on an attack and skip dinner. Breakfast was often omitted, too, by many pilots who liked to sleep in the quiet hours of the early morning, the only peaceful time of the day. The food and dysentery and malaria were what made people on Guadalcanal thin, I discovered.

After about a week, however, the officers and men of our squadron were invited over to eat with a Marine dive bombing squadron by its skipper, Lieutenant Colonel Mangrum, and there we found canned fruits and vegetables and even meat.

On October 5 we were awakened at one-thirty in the morning and told to be prepared to go on a secret mission. I was not scheduled to go, but the words "secret mission" made me so curious that I persuaded another pilot who was sleepy to let me take his place. We all gathered in Harwood's tent, shivering, while he explained that we were to make a dawn attack on Rekata Bay, on the north side of Santa Isabel Island. He pointed out that it was a very important objective. We were to hit the shore installations and then strafe and bomb the seaplanes in the bay. We were to be accompanied by about fifteen dive bombers and some Flying Fortresses. The attack was scheduled for dawn.

The idea of the attack, Bruce said, was to keep the seaplanes from taking off that morning and discovering a carrier force which intended to strike Jap installations on Bougainville, farther north in the Solomons.

We took off at three o'clock. We had some difficulty making a rendezvous, but we finally got together and headed north, with the dive bombers ahead. There were five of us.

I have never flown in such bad weather. Harwood was

flying on instrument most of the time, and the rest of us were flying contact, with only the flame of the exhaust of the plane ahead to guide us. The night was black, and the sky was covered with thick cumulus clouds.

Off the coast of Santa Isabel the clouds lowered to the water, and we flew on up the coast in soupy mist and heavy rain. Several times I lost sight of the exhaust ahead of me and had to rudder back and forth until I felt the slip stream, and then I crept slowly straight ahead until I picked the exhaust up again.

By the time we were supposed to be abreast the target there were only four out of five of us left. Shortly afterward there were only two exhausts remaining ahead of me. Then they disappeared from my sight, hard as I strained to hang on to them. Harwood told us later that he went into a power spiral and lost Taurman, pilot of the remaining plane. We were all separated.

As soon as I became lost I began to circle and wait for daylight. Then I saw some flashes of light eastward, and although I knew my target should be southward of me I set course for them. I soon realized that they were lightning flashes, however, so I continued to circle. When daylight broke I headed south until I hit the coast of Santa Isabel and then proceeded west to the target.

The first thing I saw as I approached the target was a burning plane in the water. Then I saw one of our dive bombers make a glide bomb run and come out with a float biplane on his tail. I told my gunner to watch that biplane.

The biplane left the dive bomber to tag me as I came in. I told the bomber what setup to make, checked my own switches, and then looked back. I could see my gunner's tracers—first a short burst below the following plane and then curving straight into his nose. He turned away. Hicks was a wonderful gunner and didn't need encouragement, but I couldn't resist the impulse at that moment to pick up the mike and say, "You're looking good, Hicks!"

But another biplane was approaching from the port wing and a third from the starboard. At the same time—although I didn't see him—a land-based Zero was coming in from below on our right. I told my gunner about both biplanes, and we went in over the target.

I pressed my release but, looking back, could see no bombs dropping. But I did spot the Jap anti-aircraft positions to my right rear. To my left I saw the biplane closing. I turned left and was able to complete a scissors on him before he started to shoot. As he came in overhead he rolled over on his back to keep his sights on me. I could see his tracers flicking past me but knew it was almost impossible for him to hit me in our relative positions.

I flew back over the anti-aircraft positions and pulled the emergency bomb release on my panel, as they peppered at me from below and put several holes in my wing and tail section. By that time the third biplane was on my tail, so I pushed the throttle forward and lost him.

Hicks reported that the first biplane that turned away had gone straight up and dived on us as we passed the target. Hicks shot him down. At the same time my tunnel gunner shot down the Zero closing from below.

About one third of the way back I discovered that our bombs were still on the racks. I didn't have the gas or the inclination to return at that point. I found out when I landed that the same plane had failed to release its torpedo the day before.

On the way back Hicks spotted a rubber boat ashore on a little island south of Santa Isabel, and we reported it on our return. It belonged to one of the dive bomber pilots who had been forced down there that day after enemy action. He was taken in by natives on the tip of Santa Isabel and later recovered.

The bomber and tunnel gunner who replaced Deitsch was named Struble, and it was he who shot down the Zero. He was a little fellow who looked as though he had hardly enough strength to pull a machine gun trigger. When we got back he said to me, "Gee, Mr. Mears, I didn't mean to hit that plane. I just meant to scare him. But he just caught fire and blew all to pieces." I told him I thought it would be all right this time.

When Struble pointed his gun at the Zero he probably had no idea he'd bring it down, and he was as surprised as if he'd shot his own foot when he saw it burst into flames. He got a big kick out of it when he realized what he'd done and wanted to go on every attack after that.

The attack was not a very successful one, because of the weather. Only nine navy planes and no army planes ever reached the target, and they were strung out from before dark to an hour after sunrise. However, I think the attack at least served the purpose of keeping the float planes tied to their base.

That night (October 5) we lost two of our best pilots, C.A.P. Ben Doggett and John Taurman.

Doggett and Bill Esders, of our squadron, took off after dark, each of them accompanied by a dive bomber. Their mission was to harass by bombing the landing attempts of six destroyers.

Bill told me what happened, when he returned. "I joined up on Doggett on the way back," he said. "I think he must have misread his altimeter, for I heard him say over the air that we'd better lose a little altitude, and at that time my altimeter read 1,000 feet.

"I was flying wing on him in a step-down position. Suddenly I saw the reflection of my exhaust flare in the water and pulled up violently. I looked back and saw Doggett hit the sea, bounce about 100 feet and stall off on a wing. A dive bomber circled the spot and dropped a flare not a minute afterward, but we never saw any sign of him."

Bill sprained his back when he zoomed so quickly.

Taurman became lost earlier the same night. He missed his way back to the field and, when he ran out of gas, set the plane down in the water off the southeast tip of Guadalcanal. He and the two crew members climbed into the rubber boat but found it had a hole in the bottom. They bailed all night long and next morning discovered that the current was carrying them in toward shore. When they had drifted to within about five miles of land the current began to take them out again.

One of the crew members said he thought he could make shore and dived out. He swam for six hours that day, and finally pulled himself over the coral up onto the beach. He staggered into a native village and was able to make them understand that two of his friends were still adrift. The natives paddled out in a large canoe and searched the remainder of the day, but they found no trace. Searches by plane were attempted also, from Guadalcanal, but the weather was so thick for the next few days that they were futile.

Taurman might have made the five miles ashore also, for he was a good swimmer, but he preferred to stick by his other crewmen, who couldn't swim at all.

Taurman's loss was saddening to all of us, because we knew he could have been on his way to the States if he chose. He was lost once before, after an attack on a Jap task force from his carrier in the latter part of August, and spent a month on San Cristobal Island in the Solomons. When he returned he told the squadron commander he didn't think he'd been through any great privations during his absence and therefore volunteered to remain with the squadron, even though he was to have been sent home.

Taurman told us of his experiences on the island. Because they illustrate the manner in which the natives received the American pilots, I will repeat his tale.

Taurman landed in a little bay on the north side of San Cristobal and with his crew got into the rubber boat. They had a hard time making shore because of the tide. That night they slept in shorts on the beach as best they could.

The natives, who had seen them make their water landing, appeared offshore next morning in a canoe and approached the three men standing on the beach. Taurman didn't know what island he was on, and he wasn't sure whether the natives, who were wearing machetes, were friendly or not, so he and the others just stood there and waited.

But the natives came ashore and shook hands with the three of them. Then they went back and got a large war canoe and paddled them all to their village.

They were treated very well by the natives, Taurman said. The chief of the village kicked his wife out of his hut, and the three of them lived with him. They ate bananas, coconuts, taro, sweet potatoes, and occasionally chicken. On the first night the natives killed a wild pig for them.

The three fliers spent most of the two weeks they were

with the natives on the beach watching for planes. They fired the flares they had at Flying Fortresses which passed the island, but it wasn't until they fired their last flare that one of the planes saw them. It turned and circled near them. They held up their yellow rubber boat, their life jackets, and waved. Then the plane left. They expected a navy patrol boat to come and pick them up soon.

In the meantime, they had been told by the natives of a white "headman," a "Mr. Foster," who lived on the island and had sent him a message telling him who they were. Taurman said he had thought Foster must be a missionary but that he later turned out to be the British district officer of the island.

Unfortunately, the message had been taken by a native to one village and then by another native to the next village and finally had reached Foster. When Foster received it he didn't know where it came from. But he sent one of his "soldier boys" looking for them, and this native found them two hours after the plane had sighted them.

Taurman said they waited a day for a plane to come and then paddled around the island to Kira Kira, the village where Mr. Foster lived, in a large modern house. Foster was a young Englishman of about thirty. He was glad to see them and for the next two weeks made them very comfortable. They arose in the morning about seven, drank a large glass of orange juice that was always left sitting by the bed, and then went down to breakfast. During the day they rode horseback, shot bows and arrows, and pitched horseshoes. In the middle of the morning they had an eggnog with brandy. After dinner they sipped brandy and taught Foster hearts and gin rummy.

The natives on the island had different characteristics in the different villages, according to Taurman. In one village the natives would be tall and well formed, in another they would all be suffering from yaws, and in a third they would be little and extremely ugly. The women who were apparent were all old and fat or withered, and the young girls were kept out of sight.

The three Americans were treated like heroes by the natives. Presents of fruit and food were sent to Kira Kira from villages all over the island. The natives gave a festival for them one night, in which the men performed a dance much like the hula. They sang a song about Americans saving the islands for the natives and at the end gave a "hip, hip, hurray."

Before they left the island Taurman and his crew made a tour of some of the villages, shaking hands. In one village a tall Negro came up and said, "How do you do, boys?"

Taurman was surprised and said, "He speaks English!"

"You're damn right I speak English," was the reply. "I'm an American."

His name was Ezekiel Richardson. He said he was born on Haymarket Street, in Philadelphia, and was ninety-five years old. He fought with Dewey at Manila and had his right arm cut off at the elbow. He had settled on San Cristobal twenty-five years ago and, with a partner, had started a plantation. His partner had cheated him out of his share, and then he had crossed the island and married a native woman.

Taurman's experience on the island was typical of that of many other American fliers, who often were befriended by the natives.

Our squadron commander, Lieutenant Larsen, returned to Guadalcanal on October 7 and on October 8 led us on a torpedo attack, the like of which I hope I never make again.

Four torpedo planes, seven dive bombers, and eight fighters were launched in the late afternoon to attack a cruiser and five destroyers coming down the channel. I was flying wing on Larsen.

We sighted the force while they were still only streaks on the water, and prepared to attack. We closed, and then the four of us circled from one side of the disposition to the other, just outside of anti-aircraft range, while the dive-bombers were getting into position to push over.

The five destroyers were deployed in a horseshoe about the cruiser with the open face in front. They began to wheel when they sighted us. The sun was low on the horizon as we prepared to attack, and it froze the sea with the metallic enamel of light. The ships below seemed only tiny models.

We started down from 10,000 feet when the first bomb dropped. I followed Larsen at about 300 yards. The small-caliber fire increased as we got within range, and I could see the tracers winging their way toward us. Little black puffs of anti-aircraft fire were all over the sky.

We were after the cruiser, and in order to make a run on her we had to take the fire of at least two of the five destroyers surrounding her. We came in from the port quarter of the cruiser. It was a big one and by this time had been hit by a bomb and was smoking. We paralleled it for a brief moment, and then I left Larsen and headed in to drop.

The nose of the cruiser had just poked out of the smoke when I turned. Its big, ugly snout was menacing and cruel, and as it emerged from the surrounding smoke it looked like nothing more than a dragon coming out of its cave.

Then the machine gun and small automatic fire and anti-aircraft became appalling. I kept going until it looked as though I were standing under a waterfall, so heavy was the spray which their fire kicked up. Then I dropped and turned off the bow.

Just as I turned I heard four distinct cracks. I assumed that these were made by bullets, which I could hear snapping by my face despite the roar of my motor and the fact that my ears were covered by my helmet.

The cruiser and two destroyers kept firing at me until I was at least five miles out, for what seemed an endless time.

I looked back and saw Bert Earnest following me. I had the throttle control shoved up "into the carburetor," and Bert told me later he had full gun on but couldn't catch me. Just before we cleared the Jap fire I saw one of our dive bombers burning on the water near the Jap forces.

Sometime during the run a heavy ammunition can had fallen on Struble's leg and broken it. I returned directly to base at Henderson Field without waiting to rendezvous.

Hicks reported that our radio antenna had been clipped off right before his nose, but otherwise I didn't think we'd been hit. However, when we went in for our landing and set our wheels on the mat they slowly collapsed and let the plane down on its belly.

Our planes were given credit for one torpedo hit on the attack, when several fliers agreed on seeing an explosion. We decided that Bert Earnest probably scored the hit, since he made the best run. Earnest (who flew the only one of six Grumman Avengers to return from the attack at Midway) said that the opposing anti-aircraft fire on this sortie was by far the worst he had ever encountered.

Struble was shipped out on a transport next morning. Besides his broken leg, which had been put in a cast, he was carrying a bullet scar on one shoulder. His cast was covered by the signatures of his friends. I added "Good luck for a good gunner" and gave him the rest of my cigarettes. I haven't heard of him since.

At this time we were all living in a tent camp in the Lever Brothers Cocoanut Grove, about three hundred yards from the field. During the day, when we weren't on stand-by duty at the ready tent in the middle of the field, we spent our time digging our fox holes deeper, washing clothes, playing cribbage, or bathing in the Lunga.

On October 12 we made what turned out to be my last torpedo attack from Guadalcanal. Six torpedo planes, six dive bombers, and twelve fighters hit two small enemy cruisers south of New Georgia. We concentrated on one cruiser. The attack was well timed, with the dive bombers diving first, then the fighters going in to strafe, leaving the water clear of anti-aircraft and small fire for our torpedo planes to drop.

I saw little opposing fire on this run. Nevertheless, Katz's plane was hit in the nose section and Evarts' plane in several places. We were sure of at least one torpedo hit.

Just before dark that night two of our planes were shoved off the field on a mercy mission—to drop life jackets and rubber boats to survivors of a naval battle of the night before, reported swimming off Savo Island. The report said that a large shark was idling in the water near six or seven men hanging onto a piece of debris. We saw nobody but dropped our load anyway.

11

Fox-hole Fever

FLYING FOR Torpedo Squadron Eight was brought to an abrupt halt on October 13. At one o'clock of that day twenty-seven Jap bombers moved across the sky above Henderson Field and placed their load squarely on the plane-parking area. An hour and a half later twelve more bombers came over and dropped bombs in the same spot. Our fighters were unable to intercept either enemy flight.

Only two of our torpedo planes were in flying condition after that raid.

We were up all that night.

"Washing-Machine Charlie" appeared overhead at eight-thirty and again at eleven-thirty.

Then we began to hear a new sound. It was the "whooo" of a shell whistling through the air, and then a sharp "whump" as though somebody had dumped a bucket of bolts. The explosion was on the main field.

The Japs had begun to open fire from the hills with howitzers or naval guns they somehow had succeeded in mounting. The firing was intermittent. We dubbed this new threat "Millimeter Mike."

At one-thirty on the morning of October 14 we were started from our cots by the beginning of the most intensive naval shell-fire barrage the Japs had yet laid down on Guadalcanal. I discovered later that the Japs had one battleship, three cruisers, and at least ten destroyers lobbing them in at us that night.

Five of us were in one fox hole. We huddled there crushed against the wall farthest from the opening. We could see the flash from a salvo light the sky, hear the report, then the whistle of the shells, and finally the terrible crack-crack of the shell exploding.

Coconut trees split off and crashed to the ground, shrapnel whirred through the air, a few duds came crashing and bounding through the jungle without exploding.

We smelled the powder of detonating shells. The sky was now ghostly, now brilliant with fires which had been started and with pin-wheel star shells.

Some of the shells hit not more than twenty or thirty feet from our dugout. When a big one struck, the walls of the dugout trembled the way chocolate pudding does when someone spats it with a spoon.

Ries and I were excited and were laughing, or, more exactly, giggling. Another pilot in the dugout couldn't keep himself from trembling violently every time a shell moaned by. A fourth actually was trying to burrow underneath the rest of us for protection.

The chief who was with us kept repeating three expressions involuntarily. They were "Hell's fire," "Holy balls," and "A red-ass mule."

"Don't worry, they haven't got our range yet," Ries said and half a second later had to eat his words when the top of a tree was blown into the opening of our dugout and lodged itself in the wall opposite.

This pounding continued steadily for an hour. Then there was a lull. We climbed out of our fox holes, intent on evacuating our camp area, which was being so heavily shelled.

About seventy of us were piling into a large truck assigned to the squadron, and the remainder of the men were filling up the jeeps available. Some took off on foot. We were going to the big bomb shelters near the beach.

While we were still loading into the truck the shelling began again. The truck started to roll, with men still trying to climb on the sides and running behind, begging us to stop. We stopped and started again several times, like an impatient race horse, and there were stragglers whom we had to leave.

That ride to the beach is the wildest I have ever taken, sober. Men were yelling, even crying, and trying to hide behind one another or force their way to the bottom of the truck. Some held their shirts overhead as though for protection. The truck driver was good, or he never could have taken his rolling, pitching vehicle down the road at forty miles an hour, in darkness broken only by the light of shells bursting near by.

We passed the hospital near our camp area and could see the doctors operating in the midst of shellfire.

As we neared the beach and looked out over the water we could almost make out one ship when the flash from her turrets lighted the water alongside. She was firing at one of our shore batteries.

One of the men, who thought he was being taken into an even more dangerous area, started to shout, "They're taking us down to be killed! They're taking us down to be killed!" He stopped yelling only when someone threatened to knock him off the back of the truck and made a move to do so.

The truck halted directly behind the gun position at which the Japs were shooting. We poured out of the back and streamed off into the woods toward the bomb shelters, flattening out or leaping into ditches when we saw a glitter to seaward. Once several of us jumped into a concrete-lined pit, which I found out next morning was an abandoned Jap latrine.

The shelling ceased about three o'clock, soon after we reached the bomb shelters.

Then "Washing-Machine Charlie" appeared again, and every fifteen minutes for the remainder of the night an enemy bomber dumped his load on the field and surrounding area. "Millimeter Mike" was working sporadically too.

When we crawled out of the bomb shelter the next morning, sleepy and tired, Ries gave us all a laugh by pulling the corners of his eyes toward his ears and saying, "So sorry. Which way to Henderson Field, please?"

I was still wearing a pair of blue-striped pajamas. Katz had on a raincoat, but nothing else, and several of the boys were running around in shorts. Most had been sleeping in their clothes, however.

We sent the truck down to the galley, and it returned soon with two gas cans filled with coffee. It was the sweetest-tasting nectar we could have wanted and gave everyone a lift.

We returned to survey the damage to our camp area and planes. All of our planes had been hit, and none was flyable. Our camp was not a camp any more. One tent had completely disappeared, and the only thing visible where it used to be pitched was a bomb crater. Another tent had collapsed, and all the others, along with their contents of mosquito netting, cots, tables, and papers and luggage, had been riddled and tangled and scattered by shrapnel holes and explosions. The butt plates of shells from eight to fourteen inches across were lying around.

The only thing Bert Earnest could find of his belongings was a letter he was writing to his girl, which began, "It's really not so bad here, darling."

"I guess I was just asking for it," he said.

A check on the other planes on the field revealed only five dive bombers and but a few more fighters able to fly. To us who were air-minded, the outlook for Guadalcanal was pretty black that day. When twenty-four Jap bombers came over at noon and six more later, we began to see a hopeless, losing fight. When eight planes of Bombing Six flew in late that afternoon from the New Hebrides I was almost sorry to see them come, because most of the pilots were good friends of mine.

We decided to abandon our camp area and move back with the Marines near the front lines. We issued all the squadron guns and ammunition to the men, and then, taking only the belongings and supplies we could carry, we moved to the hills and settled in a gully with a Marine special-weapons unit. We were prepared to break up into parties of eight and strike off into the hills if the Japs should make a landing and take the island.

Under the wing of the Marines our desperation subsided, however, and although we underwent several more nights of shelling we were no longer in doubt about who was going to hold the field. Major Mahoney, who led the unit we stayed with, was a professional soldier who had seen much jungle fighting in Nicaragua and was considered an expert at that type of warfare. He was a wonderful host, and even in that wild place and in those circumstances he was capable of serving good food and cigars and of making good conversation.

Another Marine officer told me he thought it would take the Japs 350,000 men to take Guadalcanal. I was glad he thought so but couldn't agree with him, in view of the status of our air power.

Our squadron, for example, did not have a single plane in flyable condition. There were three that the engineering chief thought he could repair, the least damaged one in about a week. Among the dive-bombing and fighting squadrons there was only a handful of aircraft.

Even though we couldn't fly, however, we were kept on the island, because the transports which landed and left during the next few days were packed with the badly wounded. Pilots had priority over wounded men in those planes only if they were being shipped out to bring in more planes. There were torpedo planes in the area, but there were also enough pilots available to ferry them. We stayed in order to be available to fly these aircraft if and when they arrived.

After daylight on October 15 our Douglas dive bombers and Flying Fortresses fought off Zeros to make bombing attacks on six transports off the northeast tip of the island. A PBY pilot torpedoed and sank a transport in broad daylight. All together, two transports were sunk, two set afire, and the remaining two turned back. We couldn't see the ships, but we watched the Fortresses make their runs and saw the dive bombers push over.

Our surface Navy tangled with the Jap warships and invasion forces near Guadalcanal early in the morning of October 15 and again on October 16.

On October 16 our carrier-based aircraft intercepted the enemy bombers headed for Henderson Field and shot down all sixteen.

We were able to place about six of our most jittery men aboard a destroyer on that day, in order to evacuate them. The next day ten dive bombers attacked the ship and blew off her stern. One of the men we were trying to get to safety was killed.

We spent our time during the next few days watching our fighters mix in with the Zeros and try to tag the bombers. I saw many thrilling dogfights, one so low directly overhead that I jumped into a fox hole to avoid fire. Jap bombers and Zeros continually were visible—falling, smoking, in flames, and out of control. They disintegrated on the way down and if they were high enough seemed to be in twenty pieces before they went out of sight.

During this period our engineering crew, directed by Lieutenant DeWitt Peterkin, continually exposed themselves to Jap artillery fire during the day, in an effort to repair one of the three planes we discovered we might be able to put in commission.

Major Mahoney predicted that the Japs would begin a land drive in a few days.

On October 22 our engineering crew had one plane ready to fly. Larsen took it up for a test hop, and immediately thereafter we began using it to bomb Jap artillery emplacements on the island.

The Japs had good anti-aircraft fire near their artillery positions. Twice our lone plane came back with shrapnel holes in it, and once a piece of shrapnel hit one of the bombers in the elbow.

Just at twilight on the twenty-third, Ed Hanson took the TBF up to drop bombs on a string of anti-aircraft positions and was shot down. Major Mahoney, who was riding in the plane just for the fun of it, was drowned.

Hanson said something hit his engine just after he dropped his bombs, and the engine conked and burst into flames. Fortunately, he had about 300 knots' speed and glided toward our lines. He landed in the sea, but one wheel had come down and that flipped him over on his back.

He was stunned and under water but finally managed to get out. The plane was sinking with the major, but the two crew members had been able to escape.

With Jap bullets kissing the water near their ears, Hanson and his crew swam along the shore until they saw some Marines on the beach.

"What's the password?" Hanson yelled to the Marines.

"Lucky Strike" was the answer, which was correct. Hanson and his crew swam ashore and were helped over the coral by the Marines.

The Japanese land drive started on the same night. From then until we left we slept under the continuous chatter and barking of our machine guns, rifles, mortar and howitzer fire, and the booming and pounding of our bigger guns. "Worry Willy" and "Millimeter Mike" made it more uncomfortable. Snipers broke through our lines several times, and in the daytine we heard the "kapthung" of their bullets. The snipers climbed trees and hung themselves in baskets or stretched along limbs during the night and fired in the daytime, when the flashes from their rifles could not be seen. They disguised themselves with coconut-frond coats and hats.

One night when we were trying to sleep through a hammering fire from the front lines someone came into the tent and touched me on the shoulder. "Sir, I th-th-think there's a s-s-sniper outside!" he whispered.

I said okay, charged my pistol, put my helmet on, and crept to the flap of the tent and crouched there. The person who had awakened me just then fired two shots at the sniper and scared me and everybody else in the tent within an inch of our lives.

Katz woke up, grabbed his pistol, and started waving it at me from the door. That took the fright out of me somehow and made me mad.

"God damn it, Katz, put that pistol away or I'll blow your head off!" I said; and at that point I believe I was tired and mean and irritable enough to have done so.

On October 25 the Japs started what looked like an all-out air attack. Beginning at dawn, Jap Zeros and two-engined German Messerschmitt fighters swept across the field in strafing attacks. Heavy rains on the two preceding nights made the field slushy, and our fighters were forced to wait until it dried out before they could take off.

The Jap bombers came over as usual about one o'clock.

As the day wore on, it became evident to us on the ground that there must be a Jap carrier in the vicinity. Jap Zeros were basking over the field at altitude like a school of lazy sharks. When one of our fighters would start to take off or enter the landing circle to come in, a Zero would drop down and make a pass at him. The Zeros were staying around a lot longer than they would be able to if they'd come from a land base. About three o'clock our suspicions were confirmed when eight Jap navy dive bombers with oval wings and fixed landing gear glided in for an attack on the field.

I was standing in an anti-aircraft gun emplacement near the field when the dive bombers started down. At altitude they looked as though they were coming straight for us, but when they were midway in their glide we would see they were aiming for the main landing strip.

A Marine private armed with two .45-caliber pistols was standing next to me, and he began firing as the planes came down. Both guns were blazing and roaring in my ears, and the Marine was yelling, "Yippee, yippee!" He began to follow the planes through as they pulled out and in doing so swung the pistol across my chest and fired just off my right ear. I knew the Marines were good riflemen, but I didn't trust them that much, so I jumped out and left.

October 28 was quiet in the air, because our carrier forces had engaged the Jap carrier force, and they were trading blows in another big battle (the Battle of Santa Cruz).

We were all pretty well worn out in those last days at Guadalcanal. I felt particularly sorry for a friend of mine from Boston who was still flying an SBD up the groove every day. The relief for his squadron was not due until November 15. He had been tagged by Zeros and shot up on several occasions, and the outlook for him was to keep flying until they got him. He used to come up to our camp area at night. "I dont think I can last, Fred," he would say. "Twenty days is a long time." Every time he heard guns firing his face would grow tense and he would spring forward with his ears on the alert like a hound dog. "Are those our guns? Are those our guns?" he would ask. I saw him three weeks later, when he had been relieved, and he was smiling and carefree once more, as though a 100-pound weight had been lifted from his shoulders.

Ries and I both had mild cases of dysentery then, and I think the most pleasant relaxation we had was to sit on an old three-holer near our camp overlooking the field. Basking there in the crisp of the morning or the quiet at sundown, we could chat leisurely and absorb the beauty of the jungle and mountains.

All the pilots in our squadron except the squadron commander were evacuated on October 27. We flew out in a transport carrying the severely wounded, in the early morning.

One day before we left, Ries and I walked up to the front lines and talked to some of the Marines who were fighting there. One gunner, in explaining a recent scrap, said, "I had my machine gun in a perfect position. There were Japs on all sides of me. All I had to do was swing the barrel in a circle."

"I see what you mean," Ries answered.

The stories of the heroism of the Marines on Guadalcanal are legion, but they are all well deserved.

As our transport plane clipped the top of the coconut trees on take-off in the early morning sunlight, I was thinking of those Marines. Most of them landed there on August 7 and didn't leave until the real fighting was over. It struck me that there was a good deal of truth in the last line of that verse which runs:

The Army gets the medals, the Navy gets the queens,
But the boys who do the fighting are the United States Marines.

12

Homeward Bound

THE FIGHTING FOR Torpedo Eight was not over when we left Guadalcanal. Our skipper, Lieutenant Larsen, refused to leave the island until he was properly relieved and meantime was determined to get a few more of the squadron's planes in the air, if possible. Soon after we returned to a New Hebrides port he sent word that he had managed to get ahold of three flyable aircraft and requested that some of the more rested pilots come up to man them. Bob Evarts, Larry Engel, and Bob Divine went back.

Before they returned they had seen more action. These pilots took part in sinking a large *Kongo*-class battleship which had been lying off Savo since it was crippled in a naval engagement the night before. As our boys flew in for the kill the desperate Japs fired their main 14-inch turrets, and the projectiles raised giant columns of water before the approaching planes.

Incidentally, a lot has been said of the effectiveness of these water columns in bringing down torpedo planes that I don't believe is true. I have never met anyone who has seen or heard of a torpedo plane hitting a column of sea water and flipping into the ocean, and many pilots have testified that they have flown through heavy spray at high speed without disrupting their attitude of flight.

Larry Engel told me about his attack that night. "There were plenty of torpedo planes on the island for a change," he began, "including our Marine relief and some of the boys from one of the carriers.

"The fresh pilots of these planes were making attacks on battleships sitting on the other side of Savo Island, near Guadalcanal. It had been crippled by our surface forces in the big brush the night before. They weren't getting many hits, so Swede decided we should go out, as he thought he could do better. Five TBFs and nine SBDs took off, and we were at the target in five minutes. The torpedo planes got three or four hits, and I got a probable."

Larry also told me of hammering a torpedo into a transport later that same day and then watching the ship sink—a satisfaction rarely afforded a combat aviator.

"Shortly after we speared the battleship and returned to Henderson Field a report came in placing some damaged transports in the groove between New Georgia and Santa Isabel islands. It was still morning when we took off again with four fighters and four torpedo planes. Swede and I and two of the carrier boys were carrying the torpeckers.

"We caught up with the transport and found some of them already burning from previous attacks. There were no Zeros around, and there was very little A.A. fire.

"The warships that had been escorting the transports had turned back during the night and left them as setups for us.

"One of the boys from the carrier launched his fish at one ship that was badly on fire, but unfortunately he missed. Then Swede dropped on a transport of about 10,000 tons that seemed to be in the best condition of all the vessels. It must have been manned by a skeleton crew, and if it was under way at all it had very little speed.

"I was circling and watching Swede's fish, which either was faulty or ran true and missed just astern. I saw one Jappy jump overboard after Swede dropped. Then after I was sure Swede's torpedo had missed I flew in to about 800 yards and let my torpecker go from about 200 feet. I was nosed over to about 185 knots, and after I heard the 'Torpedo away' from the radioman I pulled up and cut so I could circle the ship.

"My fish headed straight for the transport and smacked her just about amidships. The explosion was quite satisfactory and bigger than I had expected. A column of smoke and oil and debris shot up above the deck. I watched her sink—it took from seven to ten minutes—while the other pilot from the carrier flew over and pounded his torpedo into the rudder of another transport. The ship I hit went down a little at the stern and then settled slowly on an even keel.

"After letting our loads go we got together and did a little strafing to polish up the attack. There were rafts and boats all over the sea floating on an oil scum amidst chunks of wood and other stuff. There were three transports still afloat when we opened up with our guns. We strafed the transports, the boats in the water, and everything else we saw, and so did the fighters. When we turned toward Henderson Field again two of these transports were left burning fiercely and in a sinking condition, and the other one was dead in the water.

"On the way home I wondered if this little mop-up job would stop the big Jap pushes against Guadalcanal so we could go home."

Bob Evarts had the unusual experience of watching his torpedo miss one cruiser, flit past the bow of a second, and finally go home amidships on a third. The ships were in column when first sighted but turned ninety degrees into line when attacked and thereby formed a perfect mass target for a torpedo attack.

While we were waiting for the others to return we did nothing all day long except read, play cards, Chinese checkers, chess, and cribbage, and lie in the sun. Until the U.S.S. *Coolidge* was sunk after striking mines in the harbor we had at our front door on the beach a natural swimming pool formed by a wide canyon in the coral. After she went down, however, the pool filled with oil scum that clung to the rocks for days. Then our only diversion on the beach was hunting for salvage. We found, for example, a number of checkers, oars, a pair of shoes tied together, and even a full bottle of beer, the buoyancy of which puzzled us.

Bum Dope Benny spoiled a casino game for us one day by walking into the tent with a secretive air and standing there as we played. We glanced at him out of the corners of our eyes while we picked up our cards, because we were afraid he had bad news. There was a carrier in the harbor, and they lacked torpedo planes. We all hoped we were going to get a rest, but we feared otherwise.

"How would you boys like to go on a carrier?" asked Benny. The cards scattered all over the floor, and everybody stood up or flopped back and groaned. The game was broken up. Benny had just been to see a member of the staff, and he had it strictly from the inside that we were slated to go out again.

Larsen and the other three pilots were relieved by a Marine torpedo squadron on November 15 and flew in a DC-3 out of the combat zone to the island to which the remainder of us had retired.

As soon as Larsen arrived he told us we were going back to the States—in short, going home. The news was almost too good, and until we actually cleared port we couldn't believe that we wouldn't be snagged by the command and put on a carrier again. We were given our choice of traveling by air to Nouméa, thence to Hawaii, and back to San Francisco, or of going straight back to the States on a transport then at anchor in the harbor.

I chose the transport. A one-way ticket home with no stopovers was what I wanted. I was afraid a need for carrier pilots might suddenly develop in Nouméa or Pearl Harbor and I would be sent back again without first going home for Christmas. It seemed much simpler to board a ship, rest and lie in the sun on the quiet South Pacific for fifteen or twenty days, and wake up some morning off the Golden Gate than to scramble on and off transport planes for a week.

We sailed out of the harbor at sunset on November 18 with our destroyer escort. As we were leaving the bay we sighted three cruisers and several destroyers nosing into the darkening clouds to the north. War clouds, they seemed to us. Behind us we left a blaring sunset which covered the numerous islands with a profusion of shadow. Ahead lay the freedom of the seas. We were homeward bound.

As soon as we cleared the land and were once more on open water, rolling and shuddering at fifteen knots, we all relaxed and most of us went to sleep. Our cares were passed, we thought, and we had to look forward only to a fifteen-day cruise to the United States.

We were quite disappointed when we turned back that night and woke next morning off the New Hebrides again. We had returned because of official orders to pick up a Marine aircraft fighter squadron and take them back with us. We sailed again the same day.

Once more at sea, we hoped we wouldn't catch a torpedo before we got out of the danger area. The ship was nothing more than a shell and would sink in four minutes, the captain said, if a fish hit it.

The voyage across was a long, lifeless cruise. Our quarters were cramped. The ship was designed for a complement of 250 men and was carrying more than 800 now. We slept on cots on the open deck, and as we neared the States it became quite cold. We had no facilities for relaxation and most of the day did nothing but try to kill time by playing monopoly. In the evenings we all crowded into a ten-by-ten card room and flicked the pasteboards or read the old magazines. Every time someone entered the door the light blinked off to maintain the blackout. But we were going home, and we didn't mind these small discomforts. The motion of the ship and the wash of water alongside were reassuring.

Our position each day inched closer and closer on the map to the United States, and we were all anxious to get ashore and enjoy the luxuries of our country—well-dressed women, thick steaks, real ice cream, a soft, stationary bed, bright lights, a morning newspaper, cocktails, and dance orchestras. We looked forward eagerly to lapping up the advantages of civilization first and then to seeing our families.

On the morning of December 7, a year after the war began, we arrived safely back in the States. As we neared the sub nets a squadron of torpedo planes in training poured in over us like a bunch of blackbirds in a mock torpedo attack. We considered that the ship's gunners had shot them all down and proceeded through the myriads of warships and small auxiliary vessels to our berth.

Standing on the quay was Bruce Harwood, our executive officer, who had flown across and arrived before the transport. As soon as the planks hit the dock he came aboard. We all wanted to hear from him what disposal would be made of us now that we were back in the States. Were we going to go out soon? Was the squadron to be broken up? Would some of us get shore duty?

Bruce strolled up the gangway, looked us all over for a moment, then, addressing Lieutenant (jg) Jack Barnum, the senior officer present, he said, "These are your orders, Barney. Take these boys out to the nearest tavern, fill them full of beer, and report back to me in two days. That's all you need to know right now."

Who were we to argue with a superior officer?

MORE BAL-HI TITLES

U2815	**U-BOATS AT WAR**	Harald Busch	50¢
U2816	**THINGS WITH CLAWS**	ed. Whit & Hallie Burnett	50¢
U2818	**BETWEEN THE ELEPHANT'S EYES**	Robert L. Scott	50¢
U2819	**THE GERMAN RAIDER ATLANTIS**	Wolfgang Frank & Bernhard Rogge	50¢
U2820	**RE-BIRTH**	John Wyndham	50¢
U2821	**KAMIKAZE**	Yasuo Kuwahara & Gordon Allred	50¢
U2822	**THE GRAVEYARD READER**	ed. Groff Conklin	50¢
U2823	**STUKA PILOT**	Hans Ulrich Rudel	50¢
U2824	**EARTHLIGHT**	Arthur C. Clarke	50¢
U2825	**THUNDERBOLT**	Robert S. Johnson	50¢
U2826	**INDIAN COUNTRY**	Dorothy M. Johnson	50¢
U2827	**U-BOAT 977**	Heinz Schaeffer	50¢
U2828	**DEALS WITH THE DEVIL**	ed. Basil Davenport	50¢
U5800	**GREATEST FIGHTER MISSIONS**	Edward H. Sims	60¢

Write for our complete catalog:

To order by mail, send price of book plus 5¢ per book for handling to Dept. C. S., Ballantine Books, Inc., 101 Fifth Avenue, New York, New York 10003.